THE MANAGER'S POCKET GUIDE TO

Dealing with Conflict

by

Lois B. Hart, Ed.D.

HRD PRESS

Amherst, Massachusetts

Published by:

HRD Press
22 Amherst Road
Amherst, MA 01002
1-800-822-2801
(U.S. and Canada)
413-253-3488
413-253-3490 (fax)
www.hrdpress.com

ISBN 0-87425-480-9

Cover design by Eileen Klockars
Production services by CompuDesign
Editorial services by Robie Grant

Printed in Canada

TABLE OF CONTENTS

Preface

Many years have passed since I wrote *Learning from Conflict* in response to the need for trainers to help people deal with their conflicts. I frequently receive requests for an adaptation of this instructor's manual from individuals who want to learn how to handle their conflicts better but don't know how!

In the *Managers' Pocket Guide to Dealing with Conflict*, I have drawn from many people and diverse organizational settings to provide real life examples of workplace conflicts. If you are a person less than confident and successful in dealing with work conflicts, this book is for you. You will learn how to help yourself and your employees face and deal with conflicts. By dealing with these conflicts you will improve your and your employees' interpersonal relationships and improve productivity.

The seven-stage model used in this book was outlined in the 1982 edition and later the 1991 second edition of *Learning from Conflict*. The model ensures that individuals explore conflicts from many angles. We first need to recognize the messages we carry from our early years so we can identify their potency in how we deal with conflicts today. We all move into adulthood with too few skills to deal with conflicts successfully.

We also must invest some time in identifying the kinds of conflicts we have and how we react to them. No one can escape all conflicts at work, but we can control how we react to them.

It also helps to diagnose what is behind each of our conflicts in order to help resolve them. Therefore, I explore eight possible causes behind our conflicts.

Learning about our childhood conflict messages, the kinds of conflicts we have, the ways we react to them, and their causes helps to keep many conflicts from developing or escalating. This is important, because I believe we can truly avoid some conflicts entirely and decrease the growth of others. Since I personally began this work in conflict, I have considerably fewer conflicts with the people I work with and the groups I lead.

In this compact book, I have put together over twenty-five years of my experience with conflict and specific ideas on how you too can deal with your and your employees' conflicts.

Dr. Lois B. Hart
Lafayette, Colorado
October 1998

Because You're Human, You'll Have Conflicts

Conflicts occur everyday in the life of managers. You can't escape them, but you can learn how to handle them better.

What is a conflict? Conflicts are many things. They are the struggle between two or more forces, positions, or actions. For example, you have a conflict when:

- Your expectations come up against the reality of those on your staff.
- The deadline you set for a project is not met.
- People's needs for recognition are not met.
- Your work style differs from some of your staff's.
- People have hidden agendas and won't reveal their true opinions and feelings.
- Contributions are ignored so people withdraw from suggesting anything new.
- There is too much work to do and this affects personal health and family life.
- People gloss over conflicts and hope they will just go away.

Probably more than half of all people do not like conflict and will want to avoid the uncomfortable feelings associated with it. Another quarter use inappropriate methods to deal with their conflicts. This leaves very few people who confidently and successfully handle conflict. This book draws from the successful strategies used by these managers.

Unresolved conflicts are costly. Consider how much time you took to work through a recent conflict. Multiply the time by the hourly value of each person in the conflict. This total will show you the cost of one conflict.

Number of Hours per week spent on conflicts	×	Average Salary or Hourly Pay	=	Costs of Conflict
Number of Hours per week spent on conflicts	×	52 Weeks	=	Lost Time and Productivity

For instance, Robert noted that a conflict he helped resolve between two of his staff members took three hours of their time. At a prorated value of his time, this conflict cost $120 of his time plus another $90 of his two staff members'. If Robert has even two conflicts a week, this totals $21,840 a year in costs and also the loss of 312 hours!

To handle all the conflicts you face everyday, you need to learn how to:

- Identify the seven stages of the Conflict Cycle
- Apply a method of recording your conflicts

- Identify how you react to conflicts
- Name the causes of conflict
- Identify how self-interest helps us to resolve conflicts
- Learn and apply five methods for resolving conflicts
- Reflect on your conflicts and learn from each one

Most conflicts go through seven phases as shown in the Conflict Cycle. The illustration on the following page shows the seven phases:

1. Anticipation
2. Wait and See
3. Growing
4. In the Open
5. Application
6. Settlement
7. Reflection

The first phase, **Anticipation**, is the starting point. Humans, like the turtle, need a protective shield to survive. However, people know they have to stick out their necks in order to function in this world. They anticipate and expect to deal with conflicts because that is just a normal part of existence. No one relishes facing conflict, but everyone knows it will occur.

The Conflict Cycle

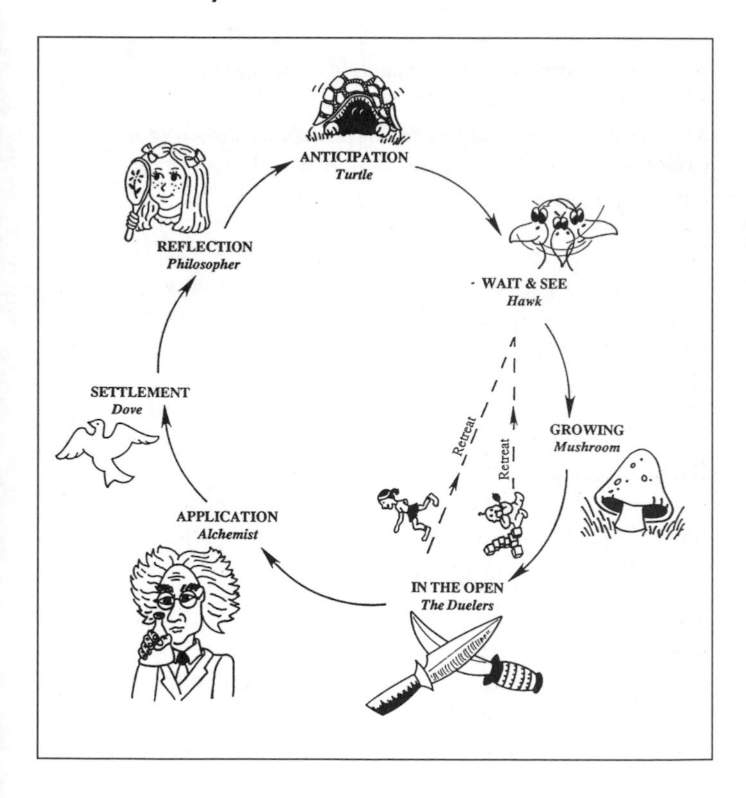

Once a conflict emerges, it moves to the second phase, **Wait and See.** Like the hawk who can fly over his territory surveying what is there, individuals also may take time in this phase to look over the situation, assess what is happening, and determine how serious it is.

Somctimes, you can resolve the conflict immediately. Sometimes, conflicts cannot be readily solved and these will mushroom into the **Growing** phase. At times, conflicts mushroom very slowly; other times they can quickly erupt into a full-scale problem, and can no longer be ignored.

Now the conflict is **In the Open** phase where there is no denying its existence. At this point, some people will **Retreat** from dealing with the conflict because they are naturally avoiders or because they want more time to assess the situation.

Once the conflict is out in the open and named, its **Resolution** is possible. As an alchemist was once able to miraculously change a thing into something even better, today we can also experiment, trying out various resolution techniques until the right one works.

The conflict moves from an **Application of Resolution** to a **Settlement** phase. The resolution occurs when everyone is satisfied. With resolution, stress and energy are redirected to other activities. Like cooing doves, the people in the conflict are ready to recapture the good feelings they previously had for one another.

The last part of the Conflict Cycle is critical although often neglected. The **Reflection** phase requires that team members reflect on the conflict they have resolved and analyze what happened so they can learn from the conflict. They ask:

- "What was the cause of this conflict and have we eliminated it so another conflict won't emerge?"
- "How did we each behave when it was obvious we had a conflict? How can we reduce our resistance to conflict?"
- "What did we do to resolve the conflict? Was it an effective method?"

Each of your conflicts will take different amounts of time to work through each phase. For instance, as lunch time rolls around, you can hardly wait to see what is on the menu. Because you are quite hungry, you immediately study the menu. You see the Philly steak and fries and think how delicious that will taste. Suddenly you remember your new commitment to eat fewer fatty foods, so you turn your attention to the salads. After lunch, you reflect on your conflict and compliment yourself on making the healthier choice. The actual amount of time for resolving your conflict might be only minutes but it went through all seven phases.

As Sondra sat down at her desk on Monday morning, she immediately felt tense as she faced the piles of work. Her first conflict of the week was how to get everything organized so it would be done within the limited hours she had.

As she scanned the work left over from the week before and the "To Do" items in her daily planner, she decided to handle a couple of the easier items quickly. She made two calls, scanned one memo, and answered five e-mails. When she looked at the clock, over an hour had passed and she still had avoided completing a prioritized list of tasks!

By postponing, she let the conflict grow. While she thought it would make her feel better to get some quick items accomplished, it actually added stress and kept the conflict alive. She should have moved the conflict in the open, reviewed her list of tasks, prioritized them, and quickly resolved the conflict with a realistic plan for the day. Sondra did reflect on this pattern of postponing the inevitable and vowed to change her ways next Monday.

Sondra's conflict remained active for about two hours. Many of our conflicts evolve over much more time before they are faced and resolved. Let's follow Elizabeth as she faces a conflict on the first day of her new job.

Phase One: Anticipation. Elizabeth expects that there will be conflicts because she has held five different jobs in the past fifteen years. During her job interview, she asked Terry, her new manager, where her work space would be. He showed her two offices. One was fully furnished with a view to the hallway. The other had only a built-in desk and chair, and was tucked back in the corner away from the door's view. Terry said they would wait until both the new hires had arrived to decide who would get which space.

Phase Two: Wait and See. Elizabeth arrived the first day on the job and immediately ran into a problem. Her new colleague, Bob, had arrived just before her and had brought a big box of books. He asked Terry where to put them and was told to chose whichever office he wanted. Naturally Bob chose the furnished office with the better location. Elizabeth's heart sank. She didn't want to make waves the first hour on the new job, however, her new office was so spartan! She also knew it was important to be visible within this male-dominated organization and she would never be seen tucked away around the bend of her space. She chose to wait and see what would happen as she and Bob met with Terry for their orientation.

Phase Three: Growing. The conflict grew. Although Bob and Elizabeth were not in their offices the first day due to other orientation activities, they needed to use them by the second day. Terry was catching up with his own work and did not seem to notice the problem about the office space. Not knowing any better, he did not intervene; if he had gotten involved the first day, the conflict could have been resolved more quickly.

By the third day, the problem had grown bigger, at least for Elizabeth. She was increasingly bothered by this inequity. She surely did not want to make waves, especially because she was only one of a few women in the organization. Bob felt some of the tension between them but thought Elizabeth was just another difficult woman. They were new to one another, so they did nothing. They could not appeal to Terry because he was away all day.

Phase Four: In the Open. As Elizabeth was reading in her office, another colleague, Sam, came in to say hello. Sam was an enthusiastic and helpful person who remembered his first few days in the organization. Sam asked Elizabeth how things were going. Initially she claimed everything was fine, but then she decided to tell Sam more. Elizabeth used this opening to tell Sam about the office problem. What a relief it was to have someone listen!

Phase Five: Resolution. Sam immediately took action to help resolve this conflict. He went across the hall and got Bob so the three of them could talk. He asked each person to describe what they ideally needed in their office. Elizabeth explained how she needed her space to be less spartan and more completely furnished. She was also concerned about keeping a high profile with the rest of the staff and Bob's set-up provided this exposure. On the other hand, she liked a quiet office as she worked on projects.

Bob said he wanted to have enough bookshelves for his books. He did not care much about the finer features of a decorated office.

Sam facilitated a discussion so they could find a solution. They decided to keep the offices they already had but with some changes.

As part of the resolution, Elizabeth decided she would intentionally walk around the department a lot during the first few months and informally stay in touch with everyone. Then later on, the staff would feel at ease poking heads around her office opening to speak to her.

Bob offered to give Elizabeth two of the art prints and the plant. Then the three of them walked around the rest of the office building looking for extra furniture. They quickly found a bookcase for Bob and two side chairs for Elizabeth.

Phase Six: Settlement. Within one hour, Elizabeth and Bob were satisfied with each of their offices and could move forward with a compatible relationship. Both Sam and Bob regularly dropped into Elizabeth's office.

Phase Seven: Reflection. Later Elizabeth reflected on this conflict. She identified that the cause was based on two different pieces of information Terry gave to Sam and her. Sam had been told on his first day to choose whichever office he wanted. She realized that their new boss should have been more aware of his miscommunication, but because he wasn't, she could have spoken to Terry on the first day.

Elizabeth also learned the value of a third party in resolving conflict. In this case another colleague, Sam, helped his two peers find a solution. She recognized how successfully Sam used negotiation to help Bob and her resolve the conflict.

How Do You View Conflict?

From the conflict messages you heard and the people you were around growing up, you developed definite beliefs about conflict.

If you experienced lots of conflicts growing up, you probably believe that conflicts are destructive and should be avoided. For you, conflict means:

- Nothing happens, there is no change in behavior or attitude.
- Energy is diverted from more important work.
- Morale is destroyed.

- People feel worse about themselves.
- People end up more polarized.
- Egos and feelings are damaged.
- Conflicts exacerbate turf wars.
- Nothing positive results from the conflict.
- You should avoid conflict as much as possible.

On the other hand, if you were exposed to adults who openly and calmly dealt with conflicts and used a variety of methods to resolve them, you probably believe that conflicts can be constructive. For you, conflict means:

- There will be a clarification of the issues.
- People feel closer after resolving the conflict.
- There is a release of tension and emotions.
- People understand and respect each other's values and experience more.
- After resolution, there is an increase in productivity.

Before you can help others deal with their conflicts, you will need to re-examine your beliefs about conflict. You will be a more effective manager if you believe conflicts are a normal and natural part of life. Some conflicts can be avoided and others can be kept from escalating. Some conflicts are not worth sweating about and others are critical to deal with. Most important, you need to take time to reflect on conflicts you've had and to learn from them so you can deal with the next conflict better.

Now that you understand the seven phases conflicts go through and have evaluated your view of conflicts, let's explore the kinds of conflicts you have to deal with in your work.

Naming Your Conflicts

Part of your success in dealing with conflicts involves taking some time to review the kinds of conflicts you have, when you have them, and with whom.

This honest evaluation is worth the effort because, in many cases, you will be able to take what you learned and avoid new conflicts in the future. For instance, you might find that you have a lot of conflicts at the same time of the day or notice you have more conflicts when you are tired. Knowing this, you can lay plans to organize your day around your energy levels.

Identifying your conflicts leads to quicker resolutions. The phrase *To name it is to claim it* means that once a conflict is named, a solution can be claimed. Named conflicts are no longer elusive, but instead manageable.

For instance, you might find that you keep having conflicts with the same person and nothing has changed. This is your red flag that it is time to get these conflicts out in the open with this person and work out those chronic issues.

The following are two methods you can use to name your conflicts. Once you complete the naming process and see its value, look for opportunities to show your staff members these techniques.

The Conflict Chart

This method involves identifying the kinds of conflicts you have with particular people in your life, both at work and in your personal life.

People	What was the conflict?	What did each do?	What was the outcome?

Use the chart shown above to develop your Conflict Chart. Down the left side of a piece of paper, list the names of people you come in contact with during a typical week. List as many as you want. Examples of people at work might be:

- your boss
- secretary
- individuals who report to you
- colleague in another department

- customers
- vendors or suppliers
- clients

To the right of each name, briefly write the conflicts you have had with each person in the recent week. What was the conflict? (Obviously you do not need to complete every line in the event you did not experience a conflict with that person.)

In the next column describe what method(s) you used to resolve the conflict. For instance, you discussed the issues until each person had a better understanding, or you negotiated a solution, or you obtained more information, or you asked your boss to intervene.

In the last column to the right, describe the outcome. For instance, you all felt relieved that the conflict was resolved, or you felt more energized for your work, or you are sleeping better. Perhaps the conflict was handled poorly and the outcomes included you felt angry still or the conflict remains.

Once you have completed the chart, you are ready to review the information, look for patterns, and decide how you can deal with conflicts differently. Turn to page 20 at the end of this chapter for some questions that will help with this clarification.

Jake is a manager in an insurance office. He wants to assess the kinds of conflicts he has and how well he handles them, so he completed the Conflict Chart for one week. Here is his chart.

People	What was the conflict?	What did each do?	What was the outcome?
Mr. Jonas (customer) and John	Mr. Jonas called to complain about John who took his claims report.	John and I reviewed the steps for handling claims.	I monitored his new claims' calls and praised him for doing it well.
My receptionist	I yelled at her for keeping a messy desk.	She became defensive and almost cried.	She called in sick the next day. Now she mopes all day.
My wife	She got on my case for playing too much golf.	She went out and spent a lot of money on clothes. I had a lousy day.	We avoid talking about it so nothing has happened.
The contractor doing the office remodeling job	We argued about the cost for fixing a mistake in the room divider.	We each argued our points, in fact quite loudly.	He won because I had signed a change order. I'm still angry.
My district manager	My monthly report showed a drop in new clients.	I reminded him of the interruptions the office had with the remodeling job. He listened.	We agreed I would get the contractor to do more of the work at night.

Before we move on to evaluating Jake's log, look over the second method you might use to name your conflicts.

For the Record

The second method for naming your conflicts involves keeping a log of your conflicts for two weeks.

Days	People	What conflict was about	What happened
1			
2			
3			
4			
5			
6			
7			
8			
9			
10			

For two weeks, you take time each day to record information about a conflict you had that day. Try to do this at the same time each day, for example, just before heading for home. Of course, if you had no conflicts some days, note this too!

In the People column, note with whom you had the conflict.

In the next column, briefly write about the conflict you have had with this person. What was the conflict?

In the next column describe what method(s) you used to resolve the conflict. For instance, you discussed the issues until each person had a better understanding, or you negotiated a solution, or you obtained more information, or you asked your boss to intervene.

At the end of two weeks you will be ready to evaluate what you recorded.

Susan is the manager of a retail store. Here is Susan's record of her conflicts for two weeks.

Days	People	What conflict was about	What happened
1	Karen, my assistant	Her tardiness . . . again	For the first time, Karen honestly explained what is happening in her personal life. We worked on a plan where she will call me ASAP when she will be late.
2	Customer	Complaint about one our new salespersons—Sara	Customer was satisfied after sounding off plus I gave her a coup-on for her next purchase. I will work with Sara later this week.

Days	People	What conflict was about	What happened
3	Vendor	Late shipment	This has been a chronic problem. I need to check the contract again and talk with our lawyer.
4	Tom, salesperson	His appearance	I noticed his clothes were not clean. We reviewed our store standards and expectations.
5	Sara, salesperson	The customer's complaint	We reviewed the steps for handling a customer's complaint. She practiced how to to word her responses to complaints.
6	Chris, cashier	I snapped at Chris when I saw him moving too slowly and there were several people in line.	I apologized to him because I did this when others might have heard. I was tired and spoke too quickly.
7	Two of my stockers	They were arguing over who was to blame about the mess in the stockroom.	I listened to both of them and together we came up with some ideas to keep the stockroom neater on a daily basis so it does not get to the point of blaming each other.

Days	People	What conflict was about	What happened
8	Landlord	Received letter re new rule about sandwich board signs outside.	Unresolved. Need to talk with other lease holders.
9	Tom	His appearance again.	I wrote up a disciplinary report for his file.
10	No conflicts today!		I am more aware of watching for growing conflicts and handled problems faster today.

What Have You Observed?

Once you have completed the Conflict Chart or For the Record log, you are ready to review the information, look for patterns, and decide how you can deal with conflicts differently. Ask yourself these questions:

1. Do you predominately have conflicts with the same types of people and rarely with others?
2. What are the usual causes of the conflicts? (You may want to review Chapter 4 on causes of conflicts.)
3. What generally worked to resolve the conflicts? What didn't? (Later you can review resolution methods in Chapter 6.)

4. What did not work? Did you make the conflict worse by going overboard, losing your temper, or becoming defensive?
5. Were the outcomes very different or similar? Were they generally positive outcomes?
6. What conclusions can you draw from reviewing this information?
7. What will you do differently the next time you face a conflict?

Jake looked over his week and realized that:

- My temper was very short this whole week.
- I had conflicts with five people, all of whom are important to me.
- I think my unresolved conflict with my wife kept me in a bad mood and then I took it out on my receptionist and the contractor.
- I think I handled the customer's legitimate complaint well and have kept it from happening again by providing additional training for John.

Susan reviewed her two weeks of conflicts and came to the following observations:

- I have conflicts with all kinds of people at work from my assistant, my salesperson, stockers, cashier, and others I depend on like my landlord and vendor.
- My conflicts are caused for many reasons: I sometimes have unclear and unstated expectations. Sara needs more

training and closer supervision. However, our vendor has serious problems with his business practices.

- Some conflicts were easy to fix, like my conflict with Chris and our customer. Others took more time, like working with the stockers.
- The problems with the vendor's late shipments will cost me more time and money if I have to go to the lawyer.
- Next time I am over stressed or overly tired, I will try to take care of my conflicts with the employees more calmly or defer them until a later or more appropriate time.
- Conflicts are certainly a natural part of this type of work. I seem to handle most of them fairly easily, but I have much more to learn.

Jake and Susan, like you, benefit from keeping track of their conflicts. The insights they gain will help them when they further analyze the causes of all of their conflicts.

The key to understanding your conflicts is to know what they are. Starting today use one of these methods to record your conflicts, who they are with, and how you handled them. With this information in hand, you will be able to review ways you react to conflicts, as described in the next chapter.

How Do You React to Conflicts?

Joe called his assistant, Lisa, into his office to discuss the report she submitted recently. With the report in front of him, Joe started going through it, page by page, pointing out the errors in the data. He criticized the logic of Lisa's conclusions, and even attacked the graphics on the report's cover.

At first, Lisa listened, nodding each time Joe made a point She took notes for awhile, but then stopped as Joe went on and on. Lisa could not hear anything clearly anymore, because inside she was thinking about how hard she had worked on this report. She silently wondered why Joe was being so critical. Occasionally she tried to defend her report, but Joe quickly interrupted her and went on.

When Joe was done, he closed the report, leaned back in his chair, looked up, and saw Lisa's reactions. Her jaw was firmly set. She did not maintain any eye contact and was blinking her eyes as if she was about to cry.

Joe was surprised by her reactions to his feedback. After all, he was just trying to be helpful so the final report would be accurate and well received! He was used to receiving critical feedback. He remembered his Army sergeant who really laid on the criticism. Joe's immediate supervisor calls him aside whenever his performance is not excellent. He wondered why Lisa was so shaken.

Reactions Are Learned Behaviors

People react to conflicts differently, some calmly and others with an explosive response. Some people flee from the conflict, and others come back fighting. Some individuals look for ways to negotiate, while others keep pushing to get their own way. Just as conflicts come in many forms, so do our reactions.

Often the way we react to conflicts is also based on how we experienced conflicts growing up. Most likely, today's reactions are based on yesterday's model. As you were growing up, how did those around you deal with conflicts? What messages did your parents, teachers, religious leaders, and scoutmasters give you?

Char was consistently told by her parents to act like a lady, which meant no fighting. She was always told, "If you can't say anything nice, then don't say anything at all."

Today, Char still reacts to conflicts just as she did as a child. She has difficulty giving any negative feedback to staff members, even when they need to correct some behavior. Instead she says nothing and this often contributes to conflicts. For instance, when she said nothing to Steve about his put-downs towards a large-sized woman in the office, her silence enraged the woman, who eventually filed a complaint with the Human Resources office.

Steve, on the other hand, had a childhood filled with loud fighting, verbal abuse, and even some physical punishment.

As an adult, Steve also yells at others when he is frustrated. He thinks his "put-downs" are only harmless teasing.

Our reactions to conflicts were learned early in our lives. These patterns are well ingrained into our adult behavior and attitudes. Fortunately we can re-learn and modify the way we react to conflicts.

Reviewing the ways you react to conflict is another piece of the puzzle for understanding how conflicts work. Often, a heightened awareness of how we react can help to keep some conflicts from escalating. We can choose how we react. We can actually learn new and better ways to react when we have conflicts.

It's in Your Body!

Whenever we are experiencing a conflict, the way we react to it will also show up somewhere in our bodies. We frequently hear about the impact stress has on our bodies. Doctors often trace high blood pressure and back pain to stress. Employers often track chronic absenteeism to unresolved problems and stress. There is always a price on our bodies when we have conflicts.

Every time Jennifer faces a conflict with a staff member, observers can always tell because she stands rigidly, tightens up her neck, and even rubs it with one hand. Once the conflict is resolved, Jennifer's neck and body relax.

Think about some of your recent conflicts. Recall what happened. Where did you feel it in your body? Did you have a reaction:

- in your head with a headache
- in your stomach with acid
- in your back with lower back pain
- in your shoulders with tightness
- in your teeth with grinding
- in your hands by biting your nails
- in your chest with tightness?

It's in the Body

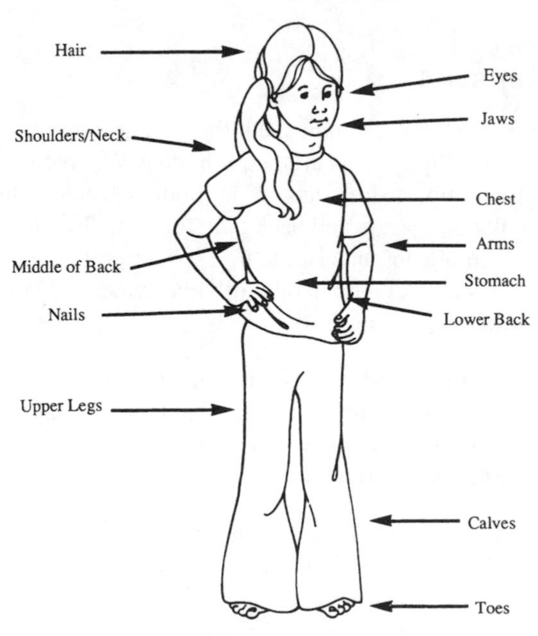

Often the clues to how we react in our bodies are in the words we use. Consider these common phrases heard as people speak about a problem:

- I'm pulling out my hair.
- You'll just have shoulder it.
- Let's bite into this problem.
- She is so stiff necked.
- I just want to close my eyes (to the conflict).
- I can't stomach any more!

These bodily reactions to conflict are automatic. The only way to change the way you react is to be aware of your behavior. Once monitored you can mitigate the power of some of your reactions.

It is important to be aware of where your reactions are stored in your body because if left unattended, your body will eventually become ill. Disease means *dis-ease*; conflicts leads to *dis-ease* in our bodies.

Are You Someone Who . . . ?

The following is a list of other ways people react to conflicts. As you review this list, note which are the types of reactions you have. Also consider if your style helps or hinders the situation.

- Do you react *defensively* with comebacks like, "You just don't understand," or "Yes, but." We often defend and justify ourselves when we feel evaluated or perceive we lack power. It also happens when we think the other person has some ulterior motive or has the authority to hurt us.

- Do you come out *fighting*? Do you respond with counter-threats or insults or seek revenge?
- Do you use *language* that is not appropriate in a professional setting?
- Do you react with either of these two extremes—very *calmly* or very *angrily*?
- Do you try to *smooth over* the conflict, emphasizing the importance of harmony and peace?
- Do you *divert* your reaction into another activity or conversation? Some people say "We won't go there" and immediately lead into another discussion. Some busily move things around or physically go for a walk.
- Do you just give in, *abdicating* by agreeing with the other person? Do you think it is hopeless and readily state, "You're right!"
- Do you *cry*?
- Do you use your *authority* to help resolve the conflict?

Look back at your Conflict Chart and For the Record logs in the previous chapter and note how you initially reacted in each conflict. Use the underlined words above to indicate your reactions in prior conflicts.

Check those conflict incidents when you reacted in an inappropriate way. Then think of what you could have done differently. (In later chapters you will learn more about alternative ways to resolve conflicts.)

Jake (the insurance office manager) reviewed his week's conflicts and immediately realized that he could not take away his fatigue, but he did not have to yell at his receptionist. Instead, he could have put aside his irritation with her messy area until another day. That way he could have chosen a time when he was rested and calmly talked the problem over with her.

Susan (the retail store manager) reviewed her two-week log and recognized that her reaction to the landlord's demand about using outdoor sandwich boards was passive. After more reflection, Susan realized that she often reacts passively to problems with people who have control or power over her. No longer is she content to continue this passive behavior. She immediately signed up for a seminar on assertiveness so she will learn how to modify this behavior.

Are You an Avoider of Conflict?

If you are an avoider of conflicts, you have plenty of company. The majority of people would rather avoid a conflict than deal with it. In fact, many of them have a very serious problem because their avoidance is so deeply engraved.

Growing up in a dysfunctional family life usually results in avoidance of conflict in adulthood. Children who observe overt conflicts, aggression, and fighting may learn quickly to avoid the pain of conflicts. As children, they felt helpless, and as adults this feeling of helplessness persists when they face new conflict situations, whether at work or in their personal lives.

Another reason we might be conflict avoiders is that there were too few models in our lives to show us how to successfully deal with conflicts. The well-meaning parents, teachers, and other adults in our lives also were inadequately prepared for adult conflicts. Even our school curriculum rarely addressed the topic of conflict. As we moved from childhood into adulthood, we came unprepared with the skills we would need to deal with conflicts. What we do not know how to do is often avoided.

So if we had poor experiences or examples of how to deal with conflicts in the past, today we may believe that conflict is bad and should be avoided at all costs. This head-in-the-sand attitude affects everyone. You will experience prolonged agony and stress over unresolved conflicts. Others around you will be frustrated by your avoidance of conflicts. It does not pay to avoid conflicts.

What Can You Do to Change Your Reactions to Conflicts?

1. Start by recognizing how you react to conflicts. Go back to your Conflict Chart or For the Record log in Chapter 2. Write down how you reacted to each conflict.
    - Is there a pattern in your reaction style or did you react differently to each conflict situation?
    - Ask yourself if your reactions were appropriate for the situation?
2. Examine your attitude toward conflict. Adjust your view of conflict from that of conflict as the enemy to that of every conflict can be an opportunity. This attitude will help you

learn more about yourself and your conflicts. Because conflicts are inevitable, you might as well benefit from each situation.

3. Work on changing your reactions slowly. Choose one of your reactions that can be changed more easily. It takes about thirty days to change a habit. Work on this one reaction for that long, monitor how well you do, then celebrate your progress. The next month, try another new behavior to replace an inappropriate reaction.
4. Seek professional help to deal with any serious avoidance to conflict pattern. This is so deep seated that a therapeutic intervention will be necessary to realize profound change.
5. Watch others' reactions to conflicts carefully. Learn to recognize your staff members' reactions by looking at the nonverbal cues they give out. Help them examine their reactions and suggest alternative ways to deal with conflicts.

Remember, we can choose how we react to conflict!

What Causes Conflicts?

Some causes of conflicts can be very simple. It is 5:30 P.M. Ted has been at work since 7:30 A.M. and was too busy to stop for lunch. He gets a phone call from one of his project managers who raises a new problem. Ted's reaction is strong. He cuts off the manager and slams down the phone.

It is not like Ted to behave so curtly, but his reaction has caused a conflict. Why? Ted is hungry! What he needs most is food, not another hour at work!

Other conflicts are more complex and their causes are harder to decipher. Jane is a new employee who feels left out and confused. This is her first professional job. After three weeks on the job, she has not produced much work. Her new boss is frustrated and upset with her. He wonders when she will begin to produce.

Jane recognizes that there are several causes to her conflict. She suspects she does not have all the information she needs to do her job well. She thinks her new boss assumes she knows more than she really does. She also is passively waiting for others to fill her in on what she needs to know. She was taught to wait for others with authority to speak to you.

Why Search for Causes to Your Conflicts?

Identifying the causes of your conflicts is an essential step in successfully resolving them. A doctor spends time diagnosing the patient's symptoms before writing a prescription. We must also diagnose what is going on so we can develop the best course of action.

Another reason for recognizing the causes of conflicts is that increased awareness will actually help some conflicts from ever developing. For instance, once Ted realized he habitually skipped lunch and realized its correlation to the conflicts he had in the afternoon, he made sure he ate regularly. Now conflicts do not happen because he is hungry.

Eight Key Causes of Conflict

The following is a quick review of eight possible causes of conflicts. As you read them, think back to some of the conflicts you named earlier in Chapter 2 and note what caused them. Later each of these causes will be explored in more detail.

1. Unmet Needs and Wants

The first cause may be within individuals and their unmet needs and wants. Conflicts happen when people are physically unwell—tired, hungry, and over-stressed. They happen when people's basic needs for recognition, affection, and affiliation are not met in their team or work environment. Can you think of a need or want you had recently that went unfulfilled? Did it lead to a conflict?

2. Values

Second, conflicts might happen because of a difference in values. Values are those beliefs that we hold dearly. Our values drive all of our behavior. People's values differ about time, money, work, health, relationships, and politics. What are one or two important values you hold? Did one of your values clash with someone else's and thus lead to a conflict?

3. Perceptions

The third source of conflicts may be differing perceptions. We all see things through different lenses that filter information based on our experiences up until this moment in time. For example, in a meeting, one person may perceive that the agenda item the team is working on is critical, whereas another may discount it as not important. Can you think of a recent occasion when you perceived a work problem differently from someone else? Did it lead to a conflict?

4. Knowledge

As in Jane's case, the information or knowledge we were given, or not given, may cause a conflict. Sometimes an individual holds a key piece of information and hoards it. This fourth cause can be easily corrected when information is available and freely shared so that everyone is "on the same page." Can you think of a time when some information was withheld and this led to a conflict?

5. Assumptions

Based on what we know, we make assumptions. Jane's boss assumed she knew more than she did. He did not check out his assumption, instead he was irritated with her low productivity. When assumptions are not discussed or checked for accuracy, they will cause conflicts. When have you made an assumption about one of your staff members and this led to a misunderstanding?

6. Expectations

The sixth cause can occur when people do not know each other's expectations. For instance, Jane expected her boss to be more helpful and not so critical. Conflicts can occur when expectations are not clarified. Jane's boss could have been clearer about what he expected of her. If expectations are shared, we can try to meet each other's expectations better. Another problem can occur when expectations are not reviewed periodically. They do change over time. When did one of your expectations lead to a conflict?

7. Growing Up Differently

A seventh cause of conflict is complex. Conflicts will occur because we all grew up differently. This cause can include the results of growing up in a particular race, ethnic, or religious group or because of our gender. Each generation views life and work differently. Each of these experiences gave us specific messages about how to deal with others and with conflicts. For instance, girls were taught to be the peacemakers and boys were encouraged to fight problems out. Jane was taught to be deferential to people in authority.

8. Willingness and Ability to Deal with Conflicts

An underlying cause that keeps people from resolving conflicts is their willingness and ability to deal with conflicts. We might not know how to deal with conflicts (our ability is lacking) so we fumble around trying to solve them. On the other hand, we may know how to deal with conflicts but are unwilling to do so.

There are many reasons why people might be unwilling to deal with conflict and thus they avoid conflict, whenever possible.

We all can learn how to deal with conflicts through reading, training, and coaching, but resistance to dealing with conflicts makes it difficult to find resolutions.

Be a Detective!

Let's see what a good detective you are! The following is a scenario in a marketing office that includes many causes of conflicts. As you read this case, mark the places where you find clues to the causes of these conflicts.

It's Friday at 4:00 P.M. Warren, the marketing manager, is reflecting on a very tough week. He's thinking,

> *"Boy, working in this department stinks! I can't get any cooperation from my boss! If he wants results, he's got to cooperate and keep me informed. I haven't got a crystal ball.*
>
> *"And why is it so hard for my staff to do their jobs right? If they want me to go to bat for them, they must keep me posted and give me more cooperation. I can't do this alone.*
>
> *"I'm ready to look for a new job. Thank God it's Friday!"*

Let's flash back to Monday morning when Warren is looking over his staff's progress reports. As he reads he thinks,

> *"Look at this report! It says that Jill's team was supposed to finish its marketing research by today but they still aren't done."*

Jill is the supervisor of the research team. Warren picks up his phone and says to Jill:

> *"I'm pretty upset that you didn't finish that report by today. What's with you, anyway?"*

Jill gets defensive and responds,

> *"Well, while you were at your doctor's appointment last Friday afternoon, your boss stopped in and ordered me to do a rush job ahead of what you asked me to do. When I explained that I had to finish this report for you by today, he yelled at me and said, 'You take orders from me! I can't have every Tom, Dick and Jill coming in here and lousing up my schedule!'"*

Warren accepted this explanation but in a chance meeting in the hallway with his boss, Bill, Warren says to Bill,

> *"Jill and I ran into a conflict when I discovered that she hadn't finished a job on time today because you asked her to do something else."*

Bill calmly stated,

> *"Warren, the job had to get done and you weren't around. I can't talk any more about this now! I'm late for a meeting. Just see that the work gets done."*

Warren scowls as he walks away,

> *"How in heaven's name can I run my department with attitudes like that?"* he thinks.

On Tuesday, Warren looks over his e-mail messages. He mutters to himself,

> *"Boy, here's a complaint from the boss. He stopped in early this morning and saw that Andy's design team left their area in a real mess."* (Andy is the supervisor of the design team.)

Warren picks up his phone and calls Andy.

> *"Hey, Andy, we've gotten a complaint from the boss about how*

messy your area looked after you left last night. I think he's upset because he has a new client visiting soon."

Andy quickly replied,

"You're right boss. We were so busy finishing that new marketing campaign that I'm afraid we ran out of time and didn't get a chance to clean up. We'll leave enough time today to do it right."

Warren was not satisfied.

"I want you do that right now! I don't want to hear any more complaints from the boss."

On Wednesday morning Warren is relieved when he checks his messages; there are no more complaints from his boss about his department. However, Andy's report showed no progress on the new marketing campaign, so Warren calls Andy again:

"Hey, Andy, what did you do yesterday . . . have a party? Your report shows very little was done on that campaign!"

Andy begins to get angry.

"Well, Warren, you wanted us to clean up the area so, that's what we did. Now you're complaining again."

"Just get the job done right!" Warren hangs up the phone with a bang and fumes!

On Thursday morning Warren is checking his messages. After reading the first one he exclaims out loud:

"He's got to be kidding! This is impossible!!!"

Warren calls Andy again.

> *"Hey, Andy, old buddy. I've got some good news and some bad news, and I need your help."*

Andy suspiciously asks,

> *"What's the problem now?"*
>
> *"The bad news is that the boss just let me know that we need to finish the design of the job sooner that we thought . . . in fact, by tomorrow instead of Monday! Your people will need to work overtime. But the good news is that he'll bring in pizza."*

Andy sighs and says,

> *"They aren't going to like this at all."*
>
> *"I know that but we have no choice,"* warns Warren.

About 3:00, Warren stops in to check on Andy's progress. Andy takes him aside and says:

> *"The team is working hard, but everyone is grumbling. Sue is going to miss her son's play at school. Tom had to find someone to pick up his kids from daycare. Sally was miffed to have to cancel a hot date she had for tonight. Sam had to tell his wife she'd have to do the grocery shopping, make dinner, and go to the 6:30 PTA meeting alone. Gee, Warren, couldn't you ask the boss to reconsider that deadline?"*

Warren did not hesitate with his answer:

> *"Look, I'm tired of all this griping. Just tell them to get the work done and I'll bring in donuts every morning next week."*

Warren thinks to himself as he walks away,

> *"They just don't get it. We have to do what the boss tells us to do. Why are they being so unreasonable?"*

Look back at your notes and see how many of the eight causes of this conflict you found in this story.

- Unmet needs and wants
- Values
- Perceptions
- Knowledge
- Expectations
- Growing up differently
- Willingness and ability to deal with conflict

Now read this interpretation from another "Conflict Detective" who evaluated the story, too.

> On Monday morning, Warren becomes irritated with his boss because he has not kept him informed. This conflict is based on unshared **knowledge**.
>
> When Warren gets irritated at Jill, this stems from his irritation with his boss. Jill feels unappreciated and undervalued, so she reacts defensively. Her **need** for appreciation is the cause.
>
> Warren's **expectation** that Jill should do what he says conflicts with Bill's expectations of Jill. Bill automatically expected Jill to do something for him without checking out the other tasks on her immediate to-do list. Bill could have talked with Jill and Warren to re-prioritize Jill's work for the coming week.
>
> Bill did not have the big picture of what work was slated for attention, nor did he ask. Jill had this **information** but chose to keep quiet. Jill's passivity may have come from messages she learned as a girl growing up. Bill's dominant behavior and know-it-all attitude could also come from messages he learned

about being a man. This conflict stems from their **growing up differently**.

Jill assumed that Bill's word was more important than Warren's. She never tested this **assumption**.

When Warren runs into Bill and Bill brushes him off, I can only guess that Warren has not felt appreciated by his boss. This cause is another **unmet need or want**.

When Warren does not feel **valued**, he probably is not in any mood to appreciate the others' work, so he tells his team to stop complaining.

When Warren calls Andy again about the delayed report, probably Warren perceived that Andy's team was goofing off. Actually they were doing what Warren expected them to do . . . clean up! So this conflict was caused by unchecked **perceptions and expectations**.

When Warren announces to his team there is an even earlier deadline, this causes a conflict with the team members' **values**. Two people had family responsibilities and another has personal social plans, whereas Warren valued meeting a deadline for a client.

In the end, when Warren gets disgusted and walks away, he is demonstrating another lesson he learned in childhood. Warren's short temper came from his childhood when his father was always spouting off without listening to his wife or children. In adulthood, Warren continued this behavior and no one challenged him on this style. This is the only way he knows how to react when he does not get his way. He clearly lacks the **ability to deal with conflict!**

In fact, we don't know enough to determine if anyone in this situation ever learned how to communicate clearly, to negotiate, or how to act as a team. If they had ever read about conflict or learned these skills in some workshop, it does not show. No one used the skills when they were most needed!

Let's Dig Deeper into These Causes!

There is more to learn about each of these eight causes of conflicts. Keep some of your conflicts in mind as you review the following.

Cause # 1—Needs and Wants are Unmet

Remember that unmet needs and wants can cause conflicts as well as when we are physically unwell, tired, hungry, and overstressed. They happen when people's basic needs for recognition, affection, and affiliation are not met.

One way to get clearer about which want or need is the basis of the conflict is to think back over the past week and recall times when some of your needs were not met. For example, perhaps you had one of the following happen to you:

- You were so hungry you snapped at your assistant.
- You were stressed out after a bad day at the office, so you failed to pay attention to your spouse, who then nagged at you.
- Your colleagues consistently ignored your suggestions in the weekly meeting. When someone else made the same suggestion, it was adopted.
- You fought an internal battle over your need to lose weight and your desire to eat the piece of cake.

Start today to become more aware of your unmet needs and wants. Try to obtain what you need immediately, especially if it is food, a break, exercise, or sleep and you will avoid some future conflicts. Pay attention to what else you want, and ask for what it is. Ask for feedback. Ask for people to give you undivided attention. Ask for some days off. What you don't ask do, you won't get!

Cause # 2—Values Are in Conflict

Conflicts often occur because of a difference in values. You can avoid many conflicts if you are clear on your values and those held by others.

Values are those beliefs that you hold so strongly that they frame your words and behaviors. For instance, Juanita's strong belief in providing a good early childhood experience prompted her to chair a company committee on starting an onsite child care center. She put her values into action.

A belief becomes a value when you are totally comfortable telling anyone about it. For instance, Michael values everyone's contributions. When a staff member interrupts another person and cuts their idea down, Michael immediately speaks up and reminds his staff that every idea has value. He even does the same when he hears colleagues discount ideas proposed in his management council. As a result of speaking out, others also have the courage to follow his example and tell others about their values.

A value is held so strongly that you would be willing to defend it. Mary values fairness and due process. When her boss went around her to promote one of her staff members, she wrote him a memo stating the importance of following the organization's procedures for promotions. She also told him that this action smacked of favoritism. He rescinded his decision.

Values are formed early in life, probably by the age of ten. Usually we adopt the values of our parents, church leaders, and teachers. Once ingrained, values are hard to change. However, when we become young adults, our childhood values do get challenged. Different values than those held by our parents are often adopted. Later in life we often will return to earlier held values. So although values are deeply ingrained, they can and do change.

We always carry our values to work. There we will find that others' values may differ from ours about time, use of money and other resources, work habits, learning and growing, health, relationships, religion, and politics. Before we can respect other's values, we need to clarify our own.

Take a little time to clarify some of your values. Write out some of your values. Try to think of values from both your personal and professional lives. For example:

"I value promptness."
"I value my time with my family."
"I value all ideas because they contribute to the best solutions."
"I value diversity."

Star any of your values that were in conflict with someone else recently.

For instance, Leslie values her family. She believes in working hard while at work but does not want to impinge on her time with her family by working extra hours. On the other hand, her boss is a workaholic and expects everyone to work overtime when he demands it. This is a conflict in values.

One way to avoid conflicts from occurring is to take time to learn about others' core values. Once you are clear on your values, take time in a staff meeting for each person to state their values. Be accepting of whatever people say is of vital importance to them.

You could go a step further and look for values that are held in common by all of the staff. This list of core values is also the foundation of your vision and mission.

Here is what one manager, Marilyn, created with her staff. They identified the values they shared in common, and then listed the beliefs they were based on. They went one step further and listed how they could put the values and beliefs into practice.

Cause # 3—Perceptions

We filter all information through our own personal lens or perceptions.

Here's a quick test to try when you attend a meeting in a different room than usually used. During the coffee break, ask each person you are standing with what their first impressions were of the meeting space and who they first saw enter the room.

Everyone will have perceived something different. Someone noticed who is wearing clothing of their favorite color. Another noticed how crowded this space seems. Most likely one person only saw what food was laid out.

Having different perceptions is normal. This works fine unless there is a conflict in perceptions. For example, a common misperception in meetings happens when the leader throws

Core Values	Based on Beliefs	Put into Practice
Diversity	Every person has worth.	We solicit and honor every person's ideas and skills.
Integrity	We believe in honesty and truth.	We do what is right—every time.
Shared Resources	Resources are there to share.	We share our resources as well as ask for what we need.
Options	There are always options available, some better than others.	Alternative options are always considered.
Social Responsibility	We live together in this world and must work together to make it better.	We build coalitions and partnerships.
Continuous Learning	Learning is a lifetime effort.	We look for every opportunity to learn.

out an issue for discussion and seeks others' ideas for solving the problem. At least half of the people will think that the leader plans to act on their suggestions when this may not be her intent at all. These individuals will enthusiastically offer ideas only to discover that their leader only intends to gather others' ideas but that she will make the final decision. This leaves these staff members frustrated and even angry.

A key to avoiding conflicts from developing is to take time to check out your perceptions with others before proceeding. In the above case, the leader can avoid misperceptions in her meetings by announcing who will be making the decision for each agenda item.

Cause # 4—Knowledge and Information

We do not have a problem when everyone has equal access to the same information or knowledge. However, in the real world information is never equally known or shared.

Some information is hoarded on purpose. Roland accepted a cross-country job. He sold his home at a loss and gave away many possessions to lighten the moving load. After two months, he and several others were laid off. He was furious. Why didn't they let him know the extent of the company's financial troubles? He had left a secure situation only to put his family in jeopardy! His boss tried to sugarcoat the reason for withholding this information, but the fact is that this act created a serious conflict.

One way to prevent conflicts is to evaluate what each person knows. Here are four categories:

1. *Information that others know and you don't know* can cause conflicts. This is what happened to Roland. No one likes surprises. A conflict can occur when a staff member suddenly announces something that affects you. For instance, Sally had a serious conflict with a customer but she did not tell her manager because she was embarrassed. Unfortunately the manager got a call from the customer and he was caught entirely off guard.
2. *Information you know but keep from others* can cause a conflict. Rich was informed by his manager that there were going to be some budget cuts. Somehow, some information leaked, and rumors started flying. Rich kept denying there were going to be cuts. Later the truth came out, and Rich's integrity was questioned.

Evaluate if you are holding back on information. Why you are keeping information from your staff? Proceed to share what you can legally and safely share. It is best to share as much as possible, as soon as possible.

3. *General knowledge is what everyone knows*. This category will not cause conflicts for you. We can help prevent conflicts by increasing the amount of knowledge we share with one another. Then everyone has what they need to get their work done.

   Set the example by sharing everything you can. (Of course, this must meet some criteria of what is appropriate.) Build a climate of trust so others will want to share information freely with you, too.

4. The last category is *information that remains hidden from everyone*. There is no sense worrying about this kind of knowledge. When it is revealed is when you will deal with it.

Cause # 5—Assumptions

Assumptions are the conclusions we draw from the information we have at hand. If these assumptions are not discussed or checked for accuracy, they will cause conflicts.

For instance, Terry read on a meeting notice there would be "light refreshments." Because the meeting started at 5:15, he assumed these refreshments would satisfy his hunger. On arrival, he found the emphasis was on "light" . . . barely enough food to feed a mouse! This created a conflict for Terry because he resented this misrepresentation. He was so hungry he could not concentrate very well.

The next time a meeting notice advertised "light refreshments" Terry picked up a burger on the way. However, at the next meeting he discovered there were large pizzas and he was not hungry! He has since learned to check out his assumptions!

Cause # 6—Expectations

The sixth cause can occur when people do not know each other's expectations. We all naturally hold expectations for ourselves and others.

Arn manages several people in their twenties. He expects all of his staff members to dress professionally. His expectation falls short on his Generation Xers who do not want to wear suits and ties. They also expect that their employer should not impinge on their personal style of dress.

Conflicts can occur when we do not clarify expectations when we start a new relationship. Arn failed to clarify the dress standard during interviews with his younger staff members. He also ignored their flagrant disregard of the dress during their first few weeks on the job. Therefore, these young people did not realize a conflict was brewing.

Conflicts also occur when we forget to review our expectations periodically. Charlotte's team carefully crafted some guidelines on how they would work together. However, they neglected to review them. Six months, then twelve months went by. Two new people were on the team and yet the guidelines gathered dust. When her team started to have more conflicts, she wondered how this happened. Then she remembered the guidelines. If she had kept them in the forefront of all of their meetings and if she had taken time with the team to review them every few months, these conflicts probably would not have grown.

Once we share our expectations, we can better meet each other's expectations.

Here is an exercise to clarify your expectations. First start by listing on the graphic an expectation that you *think* each of the following people has of you:

- Your immediate boss
- Your assistant
- Each of your staff members
- One of your colleagues

Name: ______
1.
2.
3

Name: ______
1.
2.
3

Name: ______
1.
2.
3

Name: ______
1.
2.
3

Name: ______
1.
2.
3

Name: ______
1.
2.
3

Name: ______
1.
2.
3

Name: ______
1.
2.
3

Re-read these expectations and star those that you willingly and easily can meet. For instance, your boss may expect you to behave with integrity, and you have no problem with doing this. One of your staff members expects you to inform her when she is not up to your standards working with customers, and this is fine with you.

With the remaining expectations on your list, note any that are especially difficult for you to meet. Code them with a "D." For instance, one of your colleagues expects you to go out drinking every Friday. You have children at home and a spouse who expects you there.

Next, you go to each person on your list and see if what you think they expect of you is what they actually expect. You may be surprised when you ask. As you discuss these expectations, you can also be honest about those that are difficult for you to meet. Perhaps you can re-align the expectations.

Next, write down some expectations you have of yourself. Then code each one as above; a star for those expectations you can meet for yourself and a "D" for those that are too high. Re-negotiate your own expectations.

When Lee did this he realized that he has very high expectations of himself. He thinks he should always be at the beck and call of all his staff members when they want him to be, so he has an open door policy. This causes a conflict because he never has blocks of time to do his work. The interruptions are too disruptive.

Lisa discovered she expects her reports to be perfectly written before handing them over to her assistant. This made the job easier for the assistant, but Lisa was always behind in her work. She decided to lower her standards for perfection and let her assistant take her drafts, make the corrections, and do the formatting.

This exercise can be done with your staff as well. Be sure that everyone lists their expectations privately first. Then follow up with a discussion of expectations each person holds of others in the group. Help people re-negotiate any expectations coded with a "D."

Another excellent activity to do with your staff is identify the guidelines on how you will all work together. (This is what Charlotte's team does.) The goal of this list is to identify in advance what you all can expect of one another. You can start your discussion with the sample list on page 54. Be sure to delete any that do not pertain and add any that are not included.

Once you complete your list of guidelines, have each person sign on the bottom lines. Keep the guidelines handy. Draw attention to any item when it is violated, because this keeps conflicts from escalating. Every four to six months, review your expectations.

Cause # 7—Growing Up Differently

We all grew up differently based on our race, ethnicity, gender, and even our age. We get into conflicts with one another if we come from different worlds. When we do not make the effort to learn about our differences, we will misunderstand our actions, judge, and create distance between us.

Cultural and racial differences causes conflicts when we do not respect them. For example, serious misunderstandings

Team Guidelines

- We will be as open as possible with one another.
- We will respect differences of opinion. We won't discount others' ideas.
- We will be supportive rather than judgmental.
- We will give feedback directly and openly, it will be given in a timely fashion, and we will provide information that is specific and focuses on the task and process and not on personalities.
- Because we all have resources to offer (our experiences, education, and training), we will tell others what we can offer and will contribute freely.
- We will use our time well, starting meetings on time and ending our meetings promptly.
- We will keep our focus on our goals and avoid sidetracking
- We will keep conflicts from emerging by acknowledging problems, addressing them squarely but fairly, and helping each other avoid conflicts.

Team Signatures

____________________	____________________
____________________	____________________
____________________	____________________
____________________	____________________

occur when white and African-American people do not make the effort to learn about their differences. Western business people quickly create a conflict when they do not know how Asian business people conduct business.

Men and women constantly misunderstand one another at work. A man who thinks it is gentlemanly to hold the door for a woman might be scolded by her because she wants to be viewed as strong. A woman who states her positions boldly and assertively might be viewed by men as aggressive.

Problems between generations are also the source for conflicts. Each generation experienced life differently; therefore, they hold different values. The older employee believes in loyalty to the company at all costs, whereas the younger generation thinks nothing of jumping ship often.

Neither is right or wrong . . . just different.

Identify some cultural differences between you and some of your staff members or colleagues. Identify some differences between you and a person of the other gender. Have any of these differences caused conflicts for you?

Each of these racial, ethnic, gender, and generational experiences gave us specific messages about how to deal with conflicts.

Many girls were taught to be the peacemakers. Therefore, a woman may automatically try to smooth over a conflict. Boys were encouraged to fight problems out, therefore, as men they may willingly jump in the fray.

What racial or cultural messages did you learn about dealing with conflict?

The key here is to recognize the messages we were given as we grew up. What were you told about conflict? Recall how your parents handled you and your siblings when you were fighting. Did your religion have anything to say about resolving conflicts? Can you remember any teachers who taught you how to handle conflicts with your peers?

The second key is to learn what others on your staff or team learned about conflict and to accept this. This sharing builds understanding and trust.

Cause # 8—Willingness and Ability to Deal with Conflicts

An underlying cause that keeps people from resolving conflicts is their willingness and ability to deal with conflicts.

We might not have the skills to know how to deal with conflicts. In fact, too few of us ever had a class in dealing with conflicts and interpersonal problems. Usually we learned on the playground, in high school halls, and later on the job.

In addition, we learned by example as we watched how the adults in our lives handled conflicts. Unfortunately some of these adults were inappropriate models for us to follow in adulthood.

For example, if you grew up in a dysfunctional family, one filled with emotional or physical conflicts, you probably are an avoider of conflicts today. You learned as a child that there was never a resolution to dad's drinking or mom's coldness, so as an adult you give up easily, hoping the conflict will go away.

We may know how to deal with conflicts but are unwilling to try. Perhaps you are worn out from facing too many conflicts at home, so you want a reprieve from work conflicts. Perhaps you have more important things to deal with and just wish the conflict would go away. Perhaps those childhood experiences with conflict left you with a bad taste in your mouth.

Conflicts are normal, and you must learn how to deal with them. You need to model a comfort level with dealing with conflicts. If you are a serious avoider, a therapist would be extremely helpful in overcoming this limitation. Be patient with yourself, reminding yourself that this will take time.

Some of your staff members will be avoiders, too. You know the signs if you are an avoider. Talk privately with these individuals. Listen to their concerns about facing conflicts. Challenge them gently. Ask, "How can I help you?"

Increase everyone's ability to deal with conflict. Ask your training department to schedule a workshop on conflict in your organization. Use time each week when your staff meets to try out one more idea from this book,

Improving your ability and motive to deal with conflicts takes time. Be persistent and patient. Track progress. Celebrate successes at dealing with conflict.

Use your detective skills!

You have learned about eight possible causes of conflicts. Some conflicts will be caused by one, others will be caused by several.

Use the following list as a checklist so the next time you are confronting a conflict, you can ask yourself, *Is this conflict caused by . . .*

_____ some unmet need or want?

_____ a difference in values?

_____ a difference in perceptions?

_____ a difference in knowledge?

_____ a difference in expectations?

_____ a difference in growing up differently?

_____ my willingness or ability to deal with conflict?

You Can Prevent Some Conflicts!

Some conflicts can be prevented entirely and others can be nipped in the bud. Just think of how much energy and effort you would save if you could reduce the number of conflicts you have to deal with at work. Why expose yourself to more stress than necessary when you can keep many conflicts from happening at all and other conflicts from getting out of hand? Also, you'll save your staff's time, too, if you apply some of these ideas.

Use What You Know about Your Conflicts

Throughout this book, you have been learning about the conflicts you have at work, how you react, and what causes conflicts. Many of these ideas and activities will help you and your staff prevent conflicts from developing or at least from escalating. Let's review some.

In Chapter 2, you identified the kinds of conflicts you have. You looked for patterns. From this you should now know when and where and with whom you often have conflicts. If you have asked staff people to log their conflicts, they will also know their patterns.

For instance, if you have conflicts when you are tired, overstressed, or even on certain days of the week or month, you can be extra careful at those times. Prevent conflicts by making the commitment to delay dealing with a conflict when you are most vulnerable. Postpone discussions about a conflict issue until a better time can be found for all involved.

What did you find out about where you have conflicts? Are they mostly at work and less so at home, or vice versa? What is it about the work or home situation that creates conflicts?

Maybe you are having a lot of work conflicts because you are dissatisfied with your job. Perhaps the problems with your spouse have festered too long and now the conflicts are more frequent and much more serious.

With whom do you have conflicts? Admit it, we all have some people with whom we just do not get along. Can you avoid these people? If so, stop as much contact as possible. Try to work with people whom you trust and respect and you will prevent some conflicts.

If you must work with someone you do not like or do not respect, go the extra mile to make the effort to understand them better. Go someplace away from work, perhaps over breakfast, and aim to get better acquainted on a personal level. Do not talk about work. Instead talk about your growing up experiences, schools you've gone to, what your children are like, and how you each spend your leisure time. You will probably find this person a little less difficult after you know more about his or her background and values. This alone will keep some conflicts from developing.

Use What You Know about How You React to Conflicts

In Chapter 3, you reviewed all the different ways people react when they are in a conflict. You found that some reactions were productive and some weren't. You can prevent some conflicts from escalating if you understand and monitor your reactions.

For instance, if you automatically react emotionally or defensively, come out fighting, or get angry, you can work to change these reactions. Granted, it won't be easy, but you can make these changes. One technique to use is to just stop before you react. When you feel the strong emotions rising, stop, take a deep breath, smile, get up and walk around, go get some coffee . . . do anything you can physically, *before* you speak again. This will slow down your reaction.

Another technique is to not react until you first ask some probing questions of the person you are having the conflict with. Ask, "What's really happening here?" "Can you give me an example?" When you ask for more information, you gain understanding about the causes of the conflict *and* you slow down your reaction.

As a manager, once you understand and control some of your reactions, you will be in a better position to help some of your staff who need to do the same. Just curbing strong reactions to conflicts can keep many conflicts from getting out of hand.

Use What You Know about the Causes of Conflict

Chapter 4 covered eight categories of causes behind conflicts. Through understanding each of the causes, you can prevent some conflicts from starting or growing.

First, make the effort to always stay in touch with your needs and wants. It you are conscious of them, you can seek ways to meet them. If you ignore these needs and wants, they don't go away. Instead you will find them getting them met indirectly or in inappropriate ways.

For instance, if you know about your need for approval, you can seek feedback more frequently from others so they can give you the words you need to hear. If you know about your need for food on a regular basis, you can accommodate that need and always have healthy snack food in your desk drawer or carry a small snack bag in the car.

Second, clarify your values and let others know what is important to you. Take time to ask others to share their core values. Agree to respect each other's values. This knowledge and acceptance will prevent many conflicts from ever happening.

For instance, if you value promptness and you do not let others know about this standard, you will have a conflict with people who are chronically late. If you talk with the latecomers, you may gain understanding about what is happening in their lives and what they value. From this joint understanding, you should be able to iron out a compromise and prevent future conflicts.

Third, when a conflict emerges, compare your perceptions with whomever else is involved. You may discover that this conflict is really not that serious, just a misperception. Once this is calmly cleared up, the conflict will disappear.

Fourth, open up your communications to obtain useful knowledge or information. The goal is to increase the amount of information both of you know rather than keeping it hidden. This technique will keep some conflicts from escalating.

Fifth, when a conflict emerges, check your assumptions. You may discover that this conflict is really based on the way you drew assumptions from what just happened. Once this is calmly cleared up, the conflict will disappear.

Sixth, take time to clarify and share your expectations with one another, whether it is between you and a direct report or among team members. Remember that the initial clarification is only the beginning. When people forget or neglect to review these expectations, conflict will occur. However, if you schedule time to review them periodically, you will prevent some conflicts from getting started.

Seventh, remember that the powerful messages you got growing up do not have to drive your adult life. Be selective. Review your childhood messages and choose those that are still appropriate for the present. Consciously discard the others.

Eighth, the fact that you are reading this book indicates that you are willing to learn more about how to deal with conflicts. Use this new knowledge and apply it in your everyday work. With time, you will see your comfort level about conflicts rising. You will notice there are fewer conflicts with which to deal. Of course, those around you benefit because you are modeling behaviors that others can emulate.

Hold a Conflict Trash Ceremony

Sometimes it helps to diffuse some of the anxiety over stressful problems with some humor. You can do the Conflict Trash Ceremony alone in your office. Or you can do it with your staff, especially if they have been learning together about conflict.

This ceremony works well with those less serious conflicts. The idea behind this ceremony is to discard the small conflicts, the small hurts, the small disappointments, and the small stresses . . . to let them go.

Here is how you would do it with others.

First, for one week, everyone records their conflicts on small pieces of paper.

Then when the group gets together, each individual looks over their slips and sorts them into three piles.

1. Conflicts that can easily be discarded because they are really not that important
2. Conflicts that a require minimal effort to resolve
3. More serious conflicts

Set up a ceremony with a trash can. The group stands around it with the slips of paper from the first pile of conflicts, those that are minor. One person takes one paper at a time, crumbles it up, and throws it in the can. If they wish, they can say what they want about the conflicts they are throwing away. This continues until everyone has thrown away their minor conflicts.

This ceremony should provide some relief. It will also dissipate some of the emotions that always coexist with conflicts and perhaps keep them from escalating.

If your staff works well together, they could use their problem-solving skills to help each other resolve the more important conflicts. Additional techniques for resolving conflicts are found in the next chapter.

More Ways to Resolve Your Conflicts

You may be like so many other people and think that you can jump immediately to this chapter on resolving conflicts. If you did skip the earlier chapters, go back and read them. The earlier chapters will help you understand the kinds of conflicts you normally have, how you react to them, and review eight causes of conflicts. If you skip this information, you are doing yourself a disservice and are limiting your knowledge about how to deal with your conflicts.

Once you have read the previous chapters, you are ready to look at more ways to resolve your conflicts. You have learned many ways to keep some conflicts from even starting and how some of those techniques keep other conflicts from escalating. We will not repeat those ideas here, but do not forget to periodically review what you learned about your conflict patterns, how you react to conflicts, and the causes of conflicts. All of these ideas help to resolve conflicts more efficiently, effectively, and fairly. Let's look deeper into ways you can resolve your conflicts.

What Will Help You to Resolve This Conflict?

The following method, the Force Field Analysis, is useful once you identify you want to resolve a particular conflict. This technique helps you analyze the forces that are working against and working for its resolution. Forces can include psychological, interpersonal, organizational, and societal factors.

Another way of understanding how the Force Field Analysis method works is to think about the forces both helping and hindering the flow of a mountain creek. Forces that help increase the flow would be gravity, lack of dams or boulders, and a narrow channel. Forces that would hinder the flow would be the presence of dams, boulders, and vegetation, also a very wide channel. Once we know what is keeping the water from flowing fast, we can work to eliminate the impediments.

You can use the same process for analyzing your chances of having a successful conflict resolution. The following is a description on how to use this Force Field method; an example is provided. You may want to read both parts before trying out this activity.

Force Field Analysis

Step 1 Take a piece of paper. At the top write the conflict you want to resolve. Draw a line down the middle of the paper. On the left, write *Driving Forces,* and on the other side, write *Restraining Forces*.

Conflict I Want to Resolve ____________________

Driving Forces will help ensure a resolution.	**Restraining Forces** will make it difficult to resolve.

Step 2 In the left column, list all the driving forces that will help you reach a resolution. The list of forces should include psychological, interpersonal, organizational, and societal factors.
Step 3 In the right column, list all the forces that will keep you from reaching a resolution. The list of forces should include psychological, interpersonal, organizational, and societal factors.
Step 4 Rank the restraining forces as to which are the strongest and thus most difficult to change. The goal is to first reduce those forces that have the least resistance or are the easiest to resolve.
Step 5 Also rank the driving forces as to their strength. The goal is to capitalize on those that will get the greatest changes into motion first.

For example, Randy's marriage is in trouble partly because he is working too many hours each week. He needs to work overtime because he lost two key staff members and the deadlines still need to be met. Here is his Force Field Analysis:

My conflict is that my marriage is in trouble due to too much work.

Driving Forces Will Help Resolution	Restraining Forces Make Resolution Difficult
I do not believe in divorce. The children will suffer.	My company's climate is one in which the majority of people work long hours.
My wife and I are both willing to get counseling.	The company is growing so fast that the staff cannot keep up with the deadlines.
We are currently working on filling the two job vacancies.	My boss lives for his work and not his family.
I have been developing my marketable skills in case I need to leave this job.	
I fear I will become ill or even die early if I do not get control of my hours. My father died at 55 so I am motivated to do something about this problem.	

Next Randy looked over those variables that would restrict the chances of finding a successful resolution. He ranked them and then thought about how the power of each one could be mitigated. Here is what he thinks:

#1 My boss lives for his work and not his family. This is the only restraining force I can more easily influence even though he is a workaholic. My manager knows that I do excellent work; he does not want to lose me. I can appeal to him by explaining how he would benefit if he helps me get control of my hours.

#2 The company is growing so fast that the staff cannot keep up to all the deadlines. I have some control over this variable because I am actively involved in recruiting the replacements. If I devote considerable energy here, I will get relief soon.

#3 The company climate is one in which the majority of people work long hours. I knew when I joined the company it was a group of hard-working people. Even though I will stand out as different from the rest, with my manager's help, I can change this norm for me.

Next Randy looked over those variables that would increase the chances of finding a successful resolution. He ranked them and then thought about how he could capitalize on each one.

#1 My wife and I are both willing to get counseling. This is something we can do immediately to help us adjust as I try to gain control over my work.

#2 I do not believe in divorce. Also, I fear I will become ill or even die early if I do not get control of my hours. My father died at 55. I am very motivated to do something about this problem. This will not only get me going but will sustain me as I deal with this serious conflict.

#3 We are currently working on filling the two job vacancies. Because this is already in process, this should provide me with some relief relatively soon.

#4 I have been developing more skills in case I need to leave this job. They would be quite marketable. If I cannot get my manager to cooperate, I can find another job.

From doing this analysis, Randy was able to develop an immediate plan of action before the conflict got even worse.

Within three months, the marriage counseling had made a significant difference, as he and his wife negotiated some solutions. They even took a well-needed family vacation.

He added exercise to his daily routine to help him deal with the stress and be a more pleasant spouse and father. His manager begrudgingly agreed to reduce his hours immediately. Once the two new staff people were on board, Randy reduced his hours even more.

Randy knows that without this analysis, nothing would have happened. He would have remained stuck in his conflict.

Self-Interest and Benefits

Whenever we need to change a behavior, habit, or life direction, we will be more motivated if the proposed change fits into our self-interest. We change if we know the change will benefit us in some way. We drag our feet and barely make a move in a new direction when we do not see a valid, personal reason to do so.

For instance, if we do not believe there is a good reason to change our eating habits, we will not change them.

On the other hand, if we can identify reasons that have personal meaning, we will lift our feet and skip along to a new beat. So if we find one or more very good benefits from changing eating habits, such as increased energy or lowering cholesterol, we will be more motivated to do something about it.

The same holds true for dealing with conflicts. If you have no good reason to resolve a conflict, you will not. Can you think of a conflict where you could have cared less if it ever was resolved?

On the other hand, if you find some valid reasons or benefits you will gain for resolving a conflict, you will. Can you think of a conflict that was easily resolved because it served your self-interest?

Therefore, it is helpful if you can identify how the resolution of the conflict will benefit you and the others involved in the conflict. Once each person names their self-interest or how they will benefit if the conflict is resolved, you can all readily move on to a successful resolution.

In the example described above, it was in Randy's self-interest to resolve the overtime issue because he really loves his family and wants to preserve the unit. His family gives security, love, and meaning to his life. He also does not want to get sick or die young, so it is in his self-interest to regain balance in his life.

But what about his manager and company? How will they benefit? At first glance, it appears that they would lose if Randy reduces his hours. Once the manager thought about it, he realized that it was in the company's and his self-interest to help Randy resolve this issue because he is an extremely valuable staff person, one who would be hard to replace.

Now that Randy and his manager recognize the benefits, they are ready to lay out a plan and to take action.

Fighting Fairly

Can you think of some conflict you were in when the other person did not fight fairly? We have probably all been in a situation where one person is facing a personal problem and another person comes along and picks a fight.

Linda recalls one time when she was especially vulnerable and her colleague picked a fight. She had just lost an important account and was recovering from a long bout of the flu. Sal was totally insensitive to her situation even though he knew what she had recently gone through. He went to their manager and complained about how Linda was handling one of their long-time clients. This was not a recent development, in fact, Sal had been festering about it for a long time. Just when Linda was most vulnerable, he attacked.

Can you think of some conflict situation you were in when you did not fight fairly? This is not unusual, in fact, because we are human, we can let things get out of control and act, or fight, in inappropriate ways.

Linda recalls the time she had an earlier conflict with Sal over a reporting procedure and was so angry with him that she bad-mouthed him to several other people. Afterwards, she felt terrible, but the damage was already done. She realized that she needed to learn how to fight more fairly.

Because we can expect conflicts to emerge, why not be prepared and create some agreements on how these fights will be handled? What are the ideal conditions and behaviors for handling a serious conflict?

Here is a list of some guidelines for fighting fairly that some staffs and teams have used. They reviewed this list of suggestions and adapted the wording to fit their circumstances and styles.

- When we fight, we agree to fix the problem, not assign blame, hurt, humiliate, or threaten on another. The reason this is important is that we do not want to cause even more harm by blaming, humiliating, or threatening each other.
- We agree that the timing for our fight can make a difference. We will always choose the best time to deal with the conflict. This will not be when anyone is caught unprepared, exhausted, or overwhelmed. The reason is that we want each person to feel strong, rather than vulnerable, when working on a resolution.
- If we need to postpone the time to work on the conflict's resolution, we will look for a better date to do this so the conflict does not get swept under the rug or ignored. The goal is to resolve the conflict.

- We recognize that it may appear easier to avoid dealing with the conflict. We recognize that some of us may tend to avoid conflicts so we will share the responsibility for making sure we don't avoid them. Instead, those who are avoiders will admit this and seek support from the others to change their perspective on conflict. The reason we will help each other is that if we can change our style of reacting to conflicts, we will be better equipped for dealing with future conflicts.
- We agree that sometimes we will need a mediator to help us resolve our conflict. This will be necessary when the conflict is so powerful none of us can objectively deal with it. An outsider can help us get through our fight and help us to reach an agreement.
- We agree we will use a private and even neutral location to discuss our conflict. We do not want what should be a private matter made public. This would only cause confusion and gossip.
- We agree that when a resolution is reached, we will not disclose to others the details of the process we went through, who said what, etc. This information is of no value to other people who have no direct relationship to our problem.
- We agree not to bad-mouth others or gossip about the conflict. We certainly do not want to create a new situation that could lead to yet another conflict.

Conflict Scale

Here is a very simple technique to use when a conflict is emerging. We often hear people say, "On a scale of 1 to 10 . . ." as their way to identify a degree of importance.

This Conflict Scale will help you do a quick evaluation of just how serious the conflict is and thus a way to determine if you need to take action now or later.

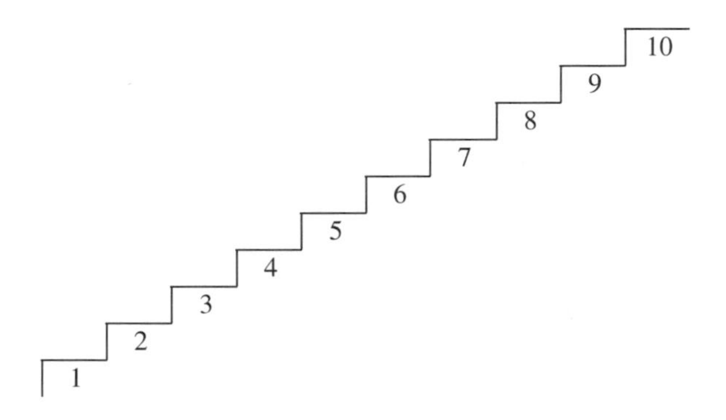

Think about a conflict as you read the following rating descriptions. Depending on the rating you choose, you will then know what to do next.

1. The conflict does not bother me nor is it really that important. I will ignore it.
2. The conflict bothers me some. I could ignore it longer.
3. The conflict is getting a little more troublesome so I could suppress it for now but will monitor the situation.

4. The conflict is starting to nag at me more since I started to monitor it.
5. This conflict is moderately upsetting to more than one of us.
6. The conflict is not going away. We better start exploring the causes.
7. We think it is worth the effort to look further into the causes.
8. The conflict is definitely affecting everyone involved. We need to work out a plan.
9. We are taking this very seriously and are ready to select the best strategy.
10. The conflict is definitely out in the open so we cannot delay. We must deal with it immediately.

If you and your staff are familiar with this scale, then when a conflict emerges each of you can assign a number to the conflict. You can agree that if one party in the conflict feels the conflict is at least two values higher than the other person's evaluation, the person assigning the lower value concedes to the other person and together they start towards a resolution.

If the person perceiving the conflict as only a 1 or 2 ignores the assessment of the other person and resists dealing with the conflict soon, this conflict will most likely grow bigger and be even more difficult to resolve later on.

Tell Me and I'll Listen

Ted has a conflict with his colleague, Ben, who turns on his conference call button and starts dialing even before the party he is calling has answered the phone. The extra loud noise wafts over the office partitions disturbing Ted's work. When Ted cannot stand it anymore, he peers over the partition and says to Ben:

> *"Why can't you be more considerate and keep your conference call button turned off? I've got important work to do!"*

Ben defensively replies,

> *"Well my work is important too so you'll just have to live with the noise!"*

As this standoff continued for several weeks, Ted and Ben were increasingly rude to one another. Helen, their manager, noticed the increased animosity and called them into her office to find out the cause.

Helen suggested she walk the men through an attentive listening process so each of them could increase their understanding of the other's positions. She first asked Ted to tell Ben why he is irritated. Ted said,

> *"I do not like it when you turn on your speaker phone button before you even know if the person you are calling is in. I am irritated by this because it disturbs me with unnecessary noise."*

Next, she asked Ted to make a statement of what he wants from Ben. So Ted continued as Ben listened:

> *"I want you to leave the speaker phone button off until you are sure the other person is in to talk with you. Actually, I wish you would go into the conference room if you need to do a conference call and not use the speaker phone in your cubicle."*

The next part was hard for Ted, but Helen asked him to make a statement of appreciation to Ben. Ted continued and told Ben:

> *"I imagine that you use the speaker phone so you can stand or walk around while you talk."*

Now Helen indicates that it is Ben's turn to talk. He had a hard time just listening and was relieved that it was his turn. But Ben was not asked to give his points, because Helen instead asked him to paraphrase what he heard Ted saying. After he did so, Ted indicated that Ben had heard him correctly.

Then Ben was asked to project what he thinks is behind Ted's complaint with a statement that starts with "I imagine you . . ."

Ben told Ted,

> *"I imagine you hate this additional noise because we already have so much noise because of these open space partitions and we all hear other people talking and walking around in our area."*

Finally Ben was asked to make a commitment as to what he could do about this conflict. Ben thought for a moment and reassured Ted that in the future he would not use his speaker phone unless he was sure Ted was out of his office. He told Ted to knock on the partition if he forgot until he changed his bad habit.

Like Helen, as a manager you might need to lead staff members who are in a conflict with one another through these steps. Until they learn the process, you will have to guide them so no step is forgotten. Actually, this technique works very well when one person serves as a mediator.

Making honest statements about a conflict and using attentive listening go hand in hand to resolve conflicts. All too often, individuals are muddled about their conflicts, and thus uneasy about stating what they feel and want from others. However, if we are not honest about our feelings and wants, we will postpone resolving some conflicts.

Here is a review of how this technique works.

Step 1 The person who has a conflict completes several of the following sentence stems that fit the conflict situation:

"I feel . . ."

"I do not like it when . . ."

"I am upset . . ."

"I am irritated . . ."

"I am annoyed . . ."

Step 2 Next, this same person completes any of the following sentence stems that pertain to this conflict:

"I want you to . . ."

"I demand that you . . ."

"I wish you would . . ."

Step 3

Then this same person tells the other what is appreciated.

"I appreciate your position . . ."

"I imagine that you . . ."

Step 4 The individual who was listening now responds by paraphrasing what he or she heard. The paraphrase is started with one of these sentence stems:

"I heard you saying . . ."

"I see you . . ."

Step 5 This person next projects what he or she thinks is behind the other person's conflict with a statement that starts with:

"I imagine you . . ."

Step 6 In the final step, this person makes a commitment as to what he or she can do about this conflict by completing one of these statements:

"I can . . ."

"I will . . ."

"I plan to . . ."

"I will try to . . ."

The Mediator

In the previous example, Helen was demonstrating a form of mediation. There are many conflict situations where two (or more) people cannot resolve their conflict because they are so embroiled and emotionally involved. Helen served as a neutral mediator to help Ted and Ben work through a conflict.

Conflicts can get resolved more easily and quickly if a neutral person would serve as a mediator. The manager should look for opportunities to help his or her staff resolve their conflicts. However, a peer can be the mediator, too.

Anyone can mediate as long as the mediator stays neutral and understands the role.

How do you mediate? The process is similar to the last technique of listening and paraphrasing. Here is an example of an office situation that benefits from a mediation conducted by a manager.

June is a well trained and experienced support person who worked herself up to this position. Howie treats June in a demeaning fashion because he has more education and perceives support staff as "slaves." June is hurt by Howie's treatment and complains to the other women, but she does not want to confront Howie.

Joseph, their manager, is probably the best person to mediate this conflict because even though he has authority over both people, they trust him.

Let's follow June and Howie through a mediation by their boss. First, he explains the ground rules.

> *"This mediation process works best when you both agree to some ground rules. You agree to follow a structured process that eventually will allow both of you time to air your complaints. This process works only if you both agree that you want it to work. Do you agree?"*

They both nod their heads in agreement. Joseph starts by asking June to state what the conflict is to Howie. She hesitates because she does not like conflict and is reluctant to make waves. With Joseph's encouragement she says,

"Howie, I know you don't intend to hurt me, but when you say demeaning remarks about my work, I feel real badly."

Howie just listens as Joseph asks clarifying questions until he is sure June has provided a complete picture.

"June, can you give Howie an example so he will know what you mean?"

June replies,

"When I gave you the last report, instead of saying thanks, you said something like, 'This sure took you long enough!'"

Then Joseph asks Howie to paraphrase what he heard June say was the problem. Once he completes his summary, Joseph asks June if Howie correctly paraphrased. June concurs it was accurate.

Now it is Howie's turn to explain his position. Joseph leads him through the same steps. Howie says,

"June, I have a lot of pressure on me to meet deadlines with my customers and I need to count on you to get the work done in a timely fashion."

Howie gives her an example of what happens when he cannot get a report to his customer on time.

June paraphrases what Howie said and even adds,

"I had no idea my late report would cause so much trouble."

Next Joseph asks both June and Howie to identify what they think is the cause behind the conflict. June shares how she has always been sensitive to negative feedback and takes it very personally. Howie recalls how he grew up in a family where the kids never got any positive feedback. He also realizes that he had withheld important information from June that could have affected her turnaround time.

Joseph adds his perceptions, too.

"I also think this problem is caused by some gender differences. I recently went to a workshop about how men and women can work better together. I learned how men generally give opinions and judgments. Like June admitted, women too often take negative feedback personally and neglect to ask for the positive feedback they need."

Once they all agree on the causes, Joseph leads a discussion of possible ways they could resolve this issue.

June and Howie each make suggestions. Their list includes:

- Howie could agree to let June know more specifically about his deadlines. June could agree to give Howie an estimate of how long it usually takes her to get reports done so Howie can turn drafts into her earlier.
- June could respond differently and deflect Howie's criticism with a statement like, "You're right, but you'll be pleased with the results!"
- Howie can make the effort to tell June at least two compliments for every complaint.

- Both can keep a log of how they give and receive feedback. Then they could review this with Joseph.
- Howie and June can attend the workshop Joseph attended on men and women working together.

They look at the pros and cons of each suggestion. They continue discussing the options until both reach consensus on a plan of action.

Once an agreement is reached, the mediator, Joseph, summarizes the agreement, suggests how their progress can be monitored, and thanks them both for cooperating.

Les has been with the company for thirty years and resents the new thirty-year-old colleague, Chris, who thinks he knows how to solve everything. Chris' confidence and enthusiasm rub Les the wrong way. Les is always putting down Chris' ideas with statements like, "We don't do it that way around here!"

In June and Howie's situation, the manager is probably the best person to mediate because the manager has authority over both people. In Les' and Chris' situation, a peer could serve as a mediator.

Can Conflicts Be Ignored?

When we ignore or deny the existence of conflicts, we usually say or do nothing and make no effort to even talk about it.

There are some occasions when it might be best to ignore the conflict. For instance, if the conflict issue is really not important to everyone involved, why waste energy on it? Let it go for now.

If the timing is wrong, wait. If you and the others in the conflict are tired, distracted by other matters, or cannot give any attention to this conflict, wait.

Also if any person is too emotional, extremely agitated, or looks like they are about to blow, stop for now. Wait until this person has calmed down, otherwise, the emotions could escalate and cause more harm.

Bridgette, a manager in the accounting department, noticed two of her staff people talking at the copier. One was criticizing the other on how she operates the machine and the second person was frowning. Bridgette decided to ignore this because she had not seen these two at odds before and trusted they could work it out if it was necessary.

Be careful though. If the conflict is important to others even though you do not think it matters, work on it now before it escalates into a worse problem. Also, conflicts that violate safety standards or your company procedures should never be ignored.

For instance, Ron had provided on-the-job training on how his workers should stack boxes in the shipping department. Even so, one person was consistently sloppy with this task. Ron realized that this unsafe practice was more important than ignoring an individual's habits. He re-trained this person immediately.

When Can Conflicts Be Smoothed Over?

When the issue is a little more important yet the timing may be off, you might smooth over the rough edges for the moment. Also, if it is important to preserve the relationships, the conflict might be played down for a while.

When we choose this method, we recognize there is a conflict, although it may not yet be very serious. In this instance, we may appeal to those in the conflict to cool off for the sake of team harmony.

Bridgette has one employee, Elliot, who has been late to work all week because his car was in the shop and he had to take the bus. When another employee began to complain about this, Bridgette smoothed it over with a short explanation and reminder that everyone needs to be flexible when there are personal emergencies.

Although we smooth the situation over, we do remain watchful. We use more time to ferret out what is causing this conflict or wait for a better time to bring the growing conflict out into the open.

Be careful though. This smoothing over method is not appropriate if the issue is quite serious and will become a crisis if ignored for too long. Work on the conflict before it becomes unwieldy.

Also move forward towards resolution and not just smoothing over if others involved in the conflict are ready and willing to work it through. They will be frustrated if you wait too long to resolve the problem.

Ron overheard one of his biggest guys ragging on a short guy. He kept an eye on both of them, watching how the harassed person handled the teasing. After this happened over a one-week period, Ron realized this issue was too important to just smooth over. The harassed person was acting more frightened. He intervened with the bully, indicating the boundaries for appropriate behaviors.

When Should I Use My Authority to Resolve Conflicts?

You use the authority and power that comes with your position as the supervisor, manager, or leader to settle a conflict between your employees when they have been unable to resolve it themselves.

Actually, that is exactly what Ron did with the harassment situation. He confirmed the company's policy on respect, and outlined what he expected and what would happen if he observed this harassment again.

Use your authority when you do have the luxury of time to help resolve the conflict.

When you are dealing with people who show little interest in fighting fairly or behave in unprofessional ways, you will have to intervene.

Be careful here, too! This is only one of many methods to resolve conflicts. If you relied only on this method, you might be viewed as a "heavy-handed boss." Also, your staff might start relying on you to resolve all conflicts when they are capable of handling many on their own. Your job is to help your employees understand their conflicts better, to recognize their choices, and use their skills in resolving their conflicts.

Is Negotiation a Good Conflict Resolution Technique?

Yes, negotiating can be very helpful in resolving some conflicts. However, many people do not know how to negotiate very well.

Negotiation requires some give and take on each person's part. Think of negotiation as a stretched rubber band. When pulled taut, the end points represent each person's starting point or position. Now release some tension on the rubber band. Perhaps it is still skewed more in one direction. Later it might relax until it is nearer the midpoint.

When we negotiate, we start with inflated positions. These positions will be in flux as we discuss the conflict. One person may give up something, while the other makes a gain. Then on another point, this may reverse. In the end, both people have changed their positions and the resolution is somewhere in the middle.

Compromise is only achieved when everyone moves off their original position to a new position that reflects the needs of all the parties. So make sure that everyone is committed to this negotiation process. Start by making sure each person's goal or position is clearly stated. Once each person has been heard by the others, begin to strive for middle ground where everyone will feel they are getting something.

Karen's team had been developing a new program for one year. It had been a struggle to get the team to work well together. She knew what each person had to offer. She had observed how well they could work together. When they were at the point of presenting the plan to the top management team, Karen was torn. She was the best speaker, however, this team had invested so much and they wanted to deliver the report. She negotiated a compromise. The team would outline the presentation and practice before a willing group of colleagues. If they did not pass this test, then Karen would use the outline but do the delivery of the report herself.

Be careful of this method also! Negotiation will not work if any person is determined to have their way and is unwilling to give up a little to reach a settlement. Some people are stubborn and do not believe in compromise. Others might have such a ridiculously inflated position that the other person will feel offended from the start.

Take Harold, for example. He is a stubborn person, with a loud mouth and very opinionated. Harold loves to argue and he never gives up his position. The staff was trying to negotiate a solution on how to allocate office space in the new building. Harold kept haranguing and complaining that he had to have the office at the end of the hall. After a while, the group gave up and just let him have his way because he would never consider a compromise.

How Does Collaboration Work to Resolve Conflicts?

Collaboration is an excellent method to reach consensus on a conflict. Use it only when those in the conflict already have a healthy respect for and trust one another. This works well with people who have successfully worked together on problems in the past.

The collaboration method requires a lot of talking through of the issue, its causes, and alternative solutions. Different from negotiation, no one starts with an inflated position. Instead, each person's values and experience are accepted. Each person is encouraged to keep talking. Talking continues until eventually a solution is found that everyone can truly live with. When this happens, they have collaborated in order to reach consensus.

Save this collaboration method for those issues that impact everyone. Use it when everyone must live with the resolution.

Here are good examples of when this method has been useful. A well-functioning staff collaborated to slice items off their annual budget. Once they were lucky when their department got extra money they had not expected. When they collaborated, they all benefited from the windfall.

Another staff put their team philosophy into practice by collaborating on the purchase of all the new office equipment. Another team used collaboration to reach consensus on how to distribute the team's recognition reward money.

Be careful when using this method! Collaborating to reach consensus takes a lot of time and patience, so use this method when everyone can invest sufficient time.

Jim had just learned about collaboration and decided to try it with his staff. Without finding out what they knew about this process nor if they even wanted to reach the decision this way, Jim charged ahead.

He posed the problem of how the sales territory was currently divided up based on seniority. He assumed they could reconfigure the territory using collaboration.

After six grueling hours, these very busy salespeople threw up their hands and revolted. They did not have the time or energy or interest in resolving the problem this way. They insisted that Jim decide! Therefore, he was left holding the bag. He was disappointed in his team. The team members were disgusted with collaboration because they found it inefficient. Looking back, Jim realized collaboration to reach consensus was the wrong method to use.

Let's Review! You have just learned more about five more methods of resolving conflicts. You could:

- Ignore the conflict.
- Suppress or smooth over the conflict.
- Use your authority to settle the conflict.
- Negotiate a resolution.
- Collaborate to reach consensus.

Read over the following two conflict situations imagining you are the manager. There are five alternatives of what you might do in each conflict. Star the alternative you most likely would do and think about why you chose it.

Next decide which conflict method is used in each of the five alternatives. Write the words, *Ignore, Suppress, Use Authority, Negotiate, and Collaborate* on the lines. (Hint: Each method is only used once in each case.)

What Would You Do?

Case #1 Peter has worked for you for over two years. In the past, he has been an exceptional employee, but lately his performance has been only marginal and other employees have complained. You know Peter wants to transfer to another department. You would:

_____ A. Tell him that if he wants to stay on the payroll, he should improve fast!

_____ B. Tell him that if he improves, you will try to get him transferred.

_____ C. Point out how his performance has been poor lately, and ask what is bothering him.

_____ D. Say nothing now; it would be inappropriate to make something out of nothing.

_____ E. Try to put the other employees at ease, because it is important that they all work well together.

I would most likely do alternative _____ because ____________________.

Case #2 As office manager, Maria encourages her employees to make suggestions for improving office procedures. On separate occasions, two of her staff approach her with different suggestions for a new filing and retrieval system. Maria sees the value of both ideas, although the suggestions are quite different. Both people think their ideas are the best. This represents just one more example of competition between them. If you were Maria, you could:

_____ A. Decide which system you will use and announce your decision to them.

_____ B. Wait and see; the best solution will become apparent.

_____ C. Tell both people not to get so uptight; this is not that important.

_____ D. Get them together and examine both of their ideas closely.

_____ E. Try one system for a quarter and then the other one, then evaluate.

I would most likely do alternative ____ because__________.

How well did you do recognizing the five methods of *Ignore, Suppress, Use Authority, Negotiate,* and *Collaborate*?

Check your answers against the following:

Case #1

- Alternative A is using your authority as the manager and telling Peter what to do.
- Alternative B is negotiation. Peter would need to change his behavior; he gives up something he is comfortable with in order to get what he wants. He will then gain something—a transfer.

- Alternative C is collaboration because it involves a lot of talking. You and Peter will discuss what is going on, look at causes, and work together to come up with a plan.
- Alternative D is ignoring. Nothing happens.
- Alternative E is smoothing over the problem with soothing words.

Case #2

- Alternative A is using a manager's authority. Maria announces her decision.
- Alternative B is ignoring. Nothing is said or done.
- Alternative C is smoothing over by telling the employees not to get upset.
- Alternative D is collaboration because everyone gets together and talks at great length about the alternative suggestions until they reach consensus.
- Alternative E is negotiation and compromise. Both ideas get tried for awhile so neither person gets their way immediately.

Looking over which alternative you chose in each case, did you choose the same method each time? If so, keep in mind that your choice of how to resolve a conflict will partly depend on what is happening in the situation. Strive to diagnose each situation and then to choose what you would do.

Use the Problem-Solving Method

Many conflicts can be resolved if you follow the five steps of a simple problem-solving method. These steps for problem solving are probably very familiar to you.

Of course, you can use this process alone, but often you will want to use this method with your staff.

This version of problem solving works best if the conflict is fairly simple.

Step 1 Write out a short statement about the conflict. Who is involved? What was said or done? When and where did this conflict emerge?

Step 2 Search for the causes. Refer back to Chapter 4 to recall all of the possible causes of conflicts. If this is a recurring conflict, identify its past occurrences.

Step 3 Set a goal . . . what do you want to happen? What does the other person want as the outcome? Is there a common goal?

Step 4 Brainstorm alternative solutions. List as many ideas as you can in a short time, without judgment.

Step 5 Select the best one or two solutions. Refine the idea and put it into practice. Later on, evaluate how it worked so you will learn from this conflict.

This chapter has shown you many methods you can use to resolve conflicts. Look back at some unresolved conflict you noted in Chapter 2 and decide which of the following twelve methods might help you to move forward:

- Force Field Analysis
- Identify Self-Interest and Benefits
- Fighting Fairly
- Conflict Scale
- Tell Me and I'll Listen
- Mediation
- Ignoring
- Smoothing Over
- Using Authority
- Negotiation
- Collaboration
- Problem Solving

7 Learning from Your Conflicts

You work is not done when the conflict is resolved. It is critical to review your experience with every conflict to determine what worked, what didn't work, and what you learned. What you learn from every conflict can help you when you face the next one. The following is one manager's conflict and what he learned.

One Team's Journey

Most groups go through several stages in their growth on the way to becoming a high performance team. You are probably familiar with this group development model: *Forming, Storming, Norming,* and *Performing*.

As suggested by the very word *Storming*, in this phase conflicts are out in the open. Clues include a noticeable increase in stress, poorer performance, or perhaps some people have withdrawn. This situation requires conflict resolution so the team can successfully move on.

Jerry's team did not anticipate conflicts when they first formed. Everyone shared a common vision and mission. Everyone was enthusiastic and ready to move forward with their tasks. Each of their earlier meetings was productive. Everyone felt a part of this newly formed team.

However, the realities of the team's project eventually did not match the original, idealistic expectations. For instance, roles were evolving and two members were not sure where they fit anymore. The project's goals expanded while the resources stayed the same.

Six months into the project, one team member, Julie, raised what appeared to be a simple question about her role. Jerry hastily and impatiently responded with his answer. Suddenly, other group members got quiet, obviously taken back by the leader's strong response. It quickly became obvious that several people had been going along with decisions even though they had reservations.

A two-hour discussion ensued. Feelings were expressed and examples given. Eventually the group realized that they had this conflict partly because they had never established team guidelines on how they would work together. Therefore, they did not have a plan in place to deal with issues as they arose. Instead, hidden agendas and concerns eventually percolated to the top months later.

Their resolution was to create a set of team guidelines. Written guidelines would keep some conflicts from ever developing in their team. They agreed to use consensus as the decision-making model because agreement by consensus would be a signal that everyone is committed to the team's efforts.

They used the general list of guidelines found on page 54. They modified, deleted, and added guidelines that fit their needs.

They wrote up a final list of guidelines, and each team member signed the agreement. They also agreed to keep the agreement "on the table" at every meeting. They rotated a Guidelines Monitor for each meeting, although they knew that ideally everyone should pay attention to the violation of any guideline.

They also set a date to review the guidelines, add to the list, and modify them as needed. If a new person joins this team, they plan to help this individual integrate more quickly with the use of these team guidelines.

So what did Jerry learn? He used the *I Learned . . .* sentence stems (from the list below) to help him answer this question.

- I was surprised that this conflict happened because the start-up of this team went so well.
- I noticed that I can get especially impatient when I am feeling stressed.
- I am disappointed that I jumped on Julie so quickly.
- I plan to use team guidelines with every new team I form.
- I learned that I can successfully resolve conflicts.

You can also use these sentence stems to stimulate your evaluation. Complete two or more of these after every conflict is resolved and you will identify the key insights you learned.

- I learned that I . . .
- I re-learned that I . . .
- I discovered that I . . .

- I noticed that I . . .
- I was surprised that I . . .
- I am disappointed that I . . .
- I plan to . . .

What Else Can You Do?

This *Manager's Pocket Guide to Dealing with Conflict* has outlined many ideas to help you understand, prevent, and resolve conflicts. Here are some final thoughts on your journey to learn from every one of your conflicts.

- Create an environment where everyone is comfortable discussing issues, stating their values, and fighting fairly.
- Lay a sound foundation with your staff or team with the use of team guidelines, a discussion of expectations, and a search for common values. This will prevent many conflicts from occurring. Include guidelines that will protect individuals from others' attacks or put-downs and a respect for everyone's contributions.
- Model how you want your staff to deal with conflict. Show them with your words and behavior. Share with them your experiences with conflict and times you have successfully dealt with conflict.
- Take time to truly understand each person's needs, values, cultural influences, gender differences, and style of handling conflicts.
- Do not avoid dealing with your conflicts. You can delay dealing with some conflicts until the timing is better, but you must face them eventually or they will only get worse.

- Review with your staff or team the Conflict Cycle in Chapter 1. When a conflict arises, evaluate together what phase the conflict is in.
- Review with your staff or team the causes of conflicts in Chapter 4 so they can gain more understanding of what is behind most conflicts.
- Learn about a variety of methods for resolving conflicts, including listening and questioning skills, negotiation, and mediation. Check the Bibliography of References for other resources on these and other topics.
- Find some ways to relieve stress and fatigue so these factors do not encourage the brewing of unnecessary conflicts.
- Be persistent and patient. It takes time, but it is worth it! You will build better relationships, reduce stress, and improve productivity.
- Track your progress. Celebrate successes when you have appropriate and timely resolutions.
- Believe there is value in learning from all your conflicts. Remain committed to your belief.

Conflicts are an inevitable part of our lives. Do not fear conflicts. You can now face them. Use all of your skills to resolve them. Always take the time to learn from them!

Bibliography of Resources on Conflict

Books

Learning from Conflict by Lois B. Hart. HRD Press, 22 Amherst St., Amherst, MA 01002 or call 1-800-822-2801. This Instructor's Manual includes workshop designs and activities.

You Just Don't Understand! by Deborah Tannen explains how the best of intentions can easily go astray.

Videos

The Art of Resolving Conflicts in the Workplace covers six techniques for smoothing over office conflicts and dealing with uncooperative co-workers. Available through Training Express, 11358 Aurora Ave., Des Moines, IA 50322.

Between You and Me: Solving Conflict shows you how to help employees solve conflicts before it affects performance. Available on CD-ROM and video through American Media Incorporated, 4900 University, West Des Moines, IA 50266 or call 1-800-262-2557.

Conflict: Managing Under Pressure shows managers how to handle conflicts caused by rumors, misinformation, differing points of view, plus identifying causes, stages, and solutions. CRM Films, 2215 Faraday Ave., Carlsbad, CA 92008 or call 1-800-421-0833.

Dealing with Conflict is based on the Thomas-Kilman Conflict Mode Instrument. Learn how to recognize and resolve conflict. Zicom Films, RR #2 Woods Rd., Tuxedo, NY 10987 or call 1-800-759-4266.

Dealing with Conflict and Confrontation shows you how to avoid temper flare ups-and one-ups-manship. In audio and video format. Available from Career Track, 3085 Center Green Drive, Boulder, CO 80301-5408 or call 1-800-223-1018.

How to Deal with Difficult People covers people such as the dictator, know-it-alls, and complainers. In audio and video format. Available from Career Track, 3085 Center Green Drive, Boulder, CO 80301-5408 or call 1-800-223-1018.

How to Resolve Conflicts on the Job covers causes, personality, how to influence others, and methods to settle disagreements. Available through Communication Briefings, 1101 King St., Suite 110, Alexandria, VA 22314 or call 1-703-548-3800.

Working with Difficult People covers several kinds of people including the overreactor, stubborn, inflexible, oversensitive, and complainer. Suggestions are given for dealing with each problem. CRM Films, 2215 Faraday Ave., Carlsbad, CA 92008 or call 1-800-421-0833.

Mixed Media

Between You and Me: Solving Conflict shows you how to help employees solve conflicts before it affects performance. Available on CD-ROM and video through American Media Incorporated, 4900 University, West Des Moines, IA 50266 or call 1-800-262-2557.

Career Track offers *Conflict Resolutions and Confrontation Skills* in both video and audio formats. 3085 Center Green Drive, Boulder, CO 80301-5408 or call 1-800-223-1018.

Feedback Instruments—Self-Administered

The Conflict Style Inventory by Marshall Sashkin assesses your own approaches to conflict management. HRD Press, 22 Amherst St., Amherst, MA 01002 or call 1-800-822-2801.

Thomas Kilman's *Conflict Mode Instrument* assesses your preferred conflict handling mode and suggestions for increasing your comfort level for the less used styles. Available from Xicom, RR #2 Woods Rd., Tuxedo, NY 10987 or call 1-800-759-4266.

Self-Study Programs

How to Manage Conflict in the Organization equips you with the strategies, tactics, and insights you need to gain control of tough conflict situations. Available from American Management Association, 1601 Broadway, New York, NY 10019-7420 or call 1-800-262-9699.

Workshop

Transforming Workplace Conflict from HRD Press shows employees how to turn conflict into a beneficial—rather than harmful—experience. Available from HRD Press, 22 Amherst Road, Amherst, MA 01002. 1-800-822-2801.

INDEX

About the Author

Lois B. Hart, Ed.D.
10951 Isabelle Road, Lafayette CO 80026
303-666-4046 Fax 303-666-4074 E-mail ihart@seqnet.net

Lois B. Hart, Ed.D. is President of Leadership Dynamics, an organization that offers workshops, individual coaching, facilitation, organizational consulting, and professional books. She is founder and Director of the Women's Leadership Insitute, a unique, year-long program of mentoring, coaching, and training for executive women.

Dr. Hart and her associates offer programs on leadership, facilitation, team development, conflict, communications, customer service, and train-the-trainer skills.

Lois has over 27 years of training, organizational development, coaching, and public education experience. She has worked with many professionals who want to be effective leaders, facilitators, and trainers. Leadership Dynamics offers training and consulting to medical and public organizations, businesses, governmental agencies, and associations that are interested in the development of their leaders and employees. Her clients include St. Joseph's Hospital, Memorial Hospital in Colorado Springs, Rapid City Regional Hospital, Washington (DC) Hospital, and Kaiser Permanente. She is consistently praised for how practical her programs are.

Dr. Hart earned a B.S. from the University of Rochester, an M.S. from Syracuse University and Ed.D. from the University of Massachusetts. Her studies included organizational behavior and leadership development with Dr. Kenneth Blanchard, co-author of *The One Minute Manager* and *Gung Ho!*

Lois has written 21 books and tapes, including *50 Activities for Developing Leaders, Moving Up! Women and Leadership, Faultless Facilitation—A Resource Guide* and *Instructor's Manual*, and *Learning From Conflict*.